Clifton College

[illegible]

Thanks

Teacher 1966-1970

ABOUT THE AUTHOR

Mark Hichens was born in London in 1926 and educated at Winchester College and New College, Oxford. He saw war service on the lower deck of the Royal Navy 1944–46. He taught general subjects in various schools in England and the United States and has always been an enthusiast for accessible, readable history. A biographer, historian and retired teacher, he has been published extensively. He lives in London.

PREVIOUSLY BY MARK HICHENS

Wives of the Kings of England: From Hanover to Windsor

Prime Ministers' Wives

Oscar Wilde's Last Chance: The Dreyfus Connection

The Inimitable P.G. Wodehouse

Queens and Empresses

Women of Consequence

The Great Performers

Abdication: The Rise and Fall of Edward V111

The Great Entertainers

The Pursuit of Truth

CAPITALISM VERSUS COMMUNISM

MARK HICHENS

Matador
9 Priory Business Park,
Wistow Road, Kibworth Beauchamp,
Leicestershire. LE8 0RX
Tel: 0116 279 2299
Email: books@troubador.co.uk
Web: www.troubador.co.uk/matador
Twitter: @matadorbooks

ISBN 978 1838594 831

British Library Cataloguing in Publication Data.
A catalogue record for this book is available from the British Library.

Printed and bound by CPI Group (UK) Ltd, Croydon, CR0 4YY
Typeset in 11.5pt Times by Troubador Publishing Ltd, Leicester, UK

Matador is an imprint of Troubador Publishing Ltd

Dedicated to Roger Fulford to whom I owe so much.

CONTENTS

FOREWORD

This book aims to give a brief but accessible account of the Cold War and the twentieth century's confrontation between capitalism and communism. It starts with the birth of communism in Europe in Karl Marx's Manifesto of 1848 and describes its imposition in Russia by the Bolsheviks under Lenin and then Stalin after the 1917 revolution. The inter-war years in Europe saw crises in capitalism, especially mass unemployment and word-wide economic recession, accompanied by the rise of Nazism in Germany under Adolf Hitler.

During the Second World War, an uneasy alliance between capitalism and communism led to the defeat of Nazi Germany. With the coming of peace, that alliance was replaced by Russian domination of Eastern Europe and the start of the Cold War. The Western powers formed the North Atlantic Treaty Organisation (NATO), to be matched by the communists with the Warsaw Pact. Former European empires in Asia disappeared while China was over-run by Mao Tse-Tung's communist forces. The 1950s and early 1960s saw occasions when world war came near in Korea, Vietnam and Cuba.

Stalin's death in 1953 changed the position of communism in Europe. His successor, Nikita Khrushchev, denounced Stalin's tyranny, cruelty and perversion of true communism although his potentially liberalising ideas were constrained by those communists who still favoured classic Marxism and repression. Khrushchev's aggressive and noisy brinkmanship led to the construction of the Berlin Wall as well as to crises in Berlin and Cuba. On his election as President of the United States in 1960, John F. Kennedy faced critical issues: in Cuba he compelled Khrushchev to withdraw his missile bases but in return had to withdraw American bases in Turkey and guarantee that the United States would not invade Cuba, thus greatly strengthening the long-term position of Fidel Castro.

In his inaugural address, Kennedy declared that Americans would pay any price to ensure the survival of liberty throughout the world but those brave words were to cause America endless trouble. As General de Gaulle foresaw, America sank into a near-bottomless military and political quagmire: the war against North Vietnam proved unwinnable and ended with America's most humiliating defeat.

In the 1970s, communism was still well-established in Eastern Europe, China and parts of south-east Asia but internal dissidents were gradually emerging. The 1980s saw a diminution of Russian power following a period of major economic decline and the unsuccessful invasion of Afghanistan. With the arrival of Mikhail Gorbachev, *glasnost* (openness) and *perestroika* (reconstruction) gradually changed the outward face of Russian communism. Gorbachev realised that if Russia was to compete with the West, freer markets and more private enterprise would be required while the Cold War involved risks that could no longer be afforded.

Ronald Reagan was elected President of the United States in 1980 with the declared intention of gaining military superiority over all America's potential enemies. He recognised Russia's growing economic weakness and the risks to world peace of continuing with the Cold War. He therefore agreed that America should take part in the Strategic Arms Limitation Talks (SALT) that eventually led to an agreement limiting the use of medium- and short-range missiles.

The fall of the Berlin Wall in 1989 saw the beginning of real change. It was followed by the unification of East and West Germany and the liberation of Eastern Europe after Gorbachev refused to use the Russian army to back their communist regimes. Democracy followed in Poland, Hungary, Czechoslovakia and Romania. In 1991, Gorbachev faced a coup from hard-line communists who were overthrown by forces led by Boris Yeltsin who thought Gorbachev had not gone far enough.

In China the course of events was rather different. In the 1960s, Mao Tse-Tung let loose the Cultural Revolution, led by the Red Guards who were to destroy much of cultural and social significance. Mao Tse-Tung also aimed to make the country a major industrial power while maintaining full-blooded communism, an approach that led to millions of deaths. Mao's successors after his death in 1976 recognised that if China was to industrialise, capitalist methods would have to be adopted – although they still adhered to Marxist-Leninism and a repressive regime, as events in Tiananmen Square were to demonstrate in 1989.

The fate of communist regimes had shown that, worthy though Marx's proclamations in his Communist Manifesto might be, his forecasts had not been fulfilled. The proletariat of the world had not united in common cause against the bourgeoisie but had shown that they would rather join it than destroy it. Gradual social reform was generally preferred to seismic revolution, while in time of war, people were ready to fight for their country rather than for abstract idealism. The truth was that beliefs cannot be imposed on people with opposition stamped out and it is beyond human capacity to create the kingdom of heaven on earth.

CHAPTER ONE

BIRTH OF COMMUNISM

Communist Manifesto – Das Kapital – First World War – Lenin – Stalin – collectivisation – reign of terror – civil war – Trotsky – Spanish Civil War – Anarchism.

Marxism-Communism came to Europe significantly in 1848 with the publication of *The Communist Manifesto*, the work of a German-Jewish scholar, Karl Marx, co-authored with Friedrich Engels. Its main theme was that history did not consist so much of wars between nations as wars between social classes – the bourgeoisie (middle), and the proletariat (workers); put plainly the 'haves' and the 'have nots'. The ills of the world – poverty, unemployment, battles – were due to the capitalist system, and attempts should be made not to improve it but to abolish it and replace it by a classless society in which there would be no private property or inheritance; education and healthcare would be free; religion would be abandoned as 'the opiate of the people'; and the central belief was to be: 'From each according to his ability, to each according to his need.' In theory it sounded unassailable.

At first, communism made no great impact. Mid-Victorian peace and relative prosperity left it on the sidelines, but it was to achieve further publicity in 1867 with the publication of Karl Marx's principal work *Das Kapital*, a resonant revolutionary thesis based, as Marx described it, 'on scientific political research.' But this is hardly an apt description. Scientific research implies seeking data, collating it, and drawing conclusions from it, instead of which Marx sought only such matter as supported his preconceived ideas of class warfare and seismic revolution. In the words of Paul Johnson[1] he was interested not so much in discovering truth as in proclaiming it. *Das Kapital* aroused widespread interest, but until the First World War it did not become an influential ideology.

Since before the outbreak of the First World War, Russia had been ripe for revolution. For years the tsars and their ministers had shown themselves incapable of governing their vast territories, although always interested in adding to them. There had been revolutionary outbreaks, but these had achieved little; they had been crushed and their leaders put to death or sent to Siberian labour camps. The supreme ruler of Russia since 1894 had been Tsar Nicholas II, feckless and incompetent; no one could have been less fitted to lead Russia into the twentieth century or to be the country's ruler in a European war. With heavy defeats of Russian armies in battle and ever increasing hardship on the home front, more frequent insurrections broke out. One occurred in March 1917 which could not be resisted when the people of Petrograd, formerly St Petersburg (later Leningrad), then the capital of Russia, starving and desperate, rioted, and the soldiers sent to suppress them joined forces with them. At the time the Tsar was at the front with his army and was prevented from

1 *Intellectuals* (Weidenfeld and Nicolson, 1988).

returning by railwaymen who stopped his train. A week later he was to abdicate.

The actual Russian Revolution came in two stages. The first had little to do with communism. After the deposition of the Tsar, power was assumed by a council of soldiers and workers known as a Soviet, most of whose leaders were moderate men pledged to continuing the war against Germany. In the following months that war was to go from bad to worse; unrest intensified and mutiny broke out in the army. And then more extreme revolutionaries arrived from abroad. These included a group from Switzerland known as Bolsheviks (meaning 'majority'). Their leader was a phenomenon with exceptional powers of leadership and great charisma. Vladimir Ulyanov (later to be known as Lenin) came from a well-to-do bourgeois family, his father an inspector of schools and he himself qualifying as a lawyer and seemingly bent on a respectable, well-ordered career; but following the execution of his elder brother for subversive activities he became increasingly involved in revolution.

He served a brief spell of imprisonment in Siberia and then for reasons of safety went into exile in Western Europe for fourteen years. On the outbreak of the First World War instead of returning to Russia to fight for his homeland, he entered into treasonous negotiations with German agents who undertook to smuggle him, with supporters, in a sealed train across Europe to Petrograd, where he would stir up discontent and make peace. In Petrograd (partly by powers of persuasion and partly strong-arm methods) he and his followers managed to gain control over the Soviet and set about the 'communisation' of the country – handing over factories to workers, land to peasants and clamping down on private enterprise.

In coming to office Lenin had promised peace with Germany and a workers' paradise based on communism. He

Vladimir Lenin. Leader of Bolshevik faction and head of government in Russia 1917–1924.

and his foreign secretary Leon Trotsky were able to obtain a separate peace treaty at Brest-Litovsk but on harsh and humiliating terms with the cession of vast areas of territory including Poland and the Ukraine. But of a workers' paradise in Russia there were few signs: food was still in desperately short supply and many thousands continued to die of starvation; to maintain the rule of communism, dictatorship of the proletariat was necessary, more despotic than that of the tsars, with no political rights for the ordinary citizen, dissidents put to death or sent off to Siberia, strict censorship imposed, conscription enforced. Forces ranged against communism were, however, powerful – dispossessed businessmen and landowners, devotees of the Russian Orthodox Church and idealists seeking freedom and democracy. Civil war between White Russians and Red was soon to break out and to last for three years.

In these circumstances Lenin realised that emergency measures were needed that were not in accordance with the doctrines of communism. And so the 'New Economic' Policy of 1921 gave more freedom to private enterprise: peasants were allowed to sell more of their surplus, more scope was given to shopkeepers and small traders, and factory workers were motivated into higher production by bonuses and piecework. To some this represented a shocking retreat from communism, but to Lenin it was unavoidable. Pure communism he did not expect to be established in his generation. He was the one man who might have led Russia out of chaos; he alone had the courage, the common sense and personal authority; but in 1922 he had the first of a series of strokes and in January 1924 he died. It is possible he might have established communism 'with a human face.' What came after him was far removed from this.

With the death of Lenin a power struggle among Bolshevik leaders was inevitable. The man whom most people expected to succeed him was Leon Trotsky who had been his right-hand man and who had won an outstanding reputation in organising the Red army during the civil war. However, the man who did emerge as Russia's new ruler was the Communist Party's General Secretary Josef Stalin who up to that time had been content to remain in the background, biding his time and stealthily building up his authority. He was different from Lenin, lacking his culture and humanity. Whereas Lenin had been the intellectual force behind the Revolution, Stalin had been one of the principal hit-men, staging hold-ups and murders and organising blackmail and 'protection' payments. Cunning, suspicious and utterly ruthless, he was to become one of Russia's most powerful and terrifying rulers, but it was he who, regardless of human suffering and loss of life, was to make Russia a great world power.

Stalin was born in Georgia in the south, which had only become part of Russia in the nineteenth century and where anti-Russian feeling was still strong. His parents were impoverished; his father, an ex-serf, earned a precarious living as a cobbler, most of which he spent on drink; he had no love for his son and treated him brutally. His mother, a deeply religious woman, took in sewing and washing and worked as hard as she could to support her only child; her great ambition was that he should become a priest and by dint of hard work and self-sacrifice she was able to scrape together enough money for him to go to a theological college, but it became clear soon that Josef was not cut out for priesthood and after a short time he was expelled. From then he became more and more involved in revolutionary movements and was often in prison, although he does not seem to have played a leading part in the revolutions of 1917. He was, however, given a position by Lenin in his government in that year from which he later gained the key position of general secretary

Josef Stalin. General secretary of the Communist Party of the Soviet Union and dictator of Russia 1924–1953.

of the party and was able to manoeuvre himself as head of state after Lenin's death. Before he died Lenin had foreseen that this might happen and had tried to prevent it. He wrote: 'Stalin, having become general secretary has concentrated enormous power in his hands. I am not sure he knows how to use that power with sufficient caution. He is too rude. I propose that the comrades find a way to remove Stalin from the position and appoint another man.' But incapacitated as Lenin was by then, he was unable to check him and once in power Stalin could not be shifted.

It was never likely that Stalin and Trotsky would be able to work together; their temperaments clashed violently and they disagreed strongly on one fundamental matter. Trotsky was convinced that the communist revolution should be spread into other countries, and that only thus would it be successful in Russia. Stalin on the other hand maintained that other countries were not their concern and that it was the duty of Russian communists to build up Russian strength and make the country a great world power. In time it was Stalin who was to prevail, while Trotsky was driven into exile, denounced as the greatest traitor of all time and later assassinated in Mexico.

Once installed in power Stalin soon realised that if Russia was to become the great power he envisaged, there would have to be further sacrifices of communism: equality, freedom and human rights would have to go by the board. A new class of highly privileged technocrats, administrators, policemen and espionage agents would have to be brought into existence. For the time being a classless society was out of the question.

It was to be in agriculture that Stalin was to enforce communism at its most ruthless and brutal. It was soon to become evident that an agricultural system based on peasants' smallholdings was inefficient and incapable of providing enough food for the growing population of the towns. Peasants were inclined to produce only slightly more than their own needs and were unable and unwilling to introduce new machinery and scientific methods. There had to be collectivisation – that is, smallholdings swept away and brought into large-scale cooperatives regardless of human suffering and loss of life. The first to be expropriated were the Kulaks, peasants with larger holdings. As these were prepared to resist collectivisation to the death, Stalin decided that they should be exterminated. Accordingly, they were driven from their farms. Some were shot on the spot, some were packed off to Siberia, some left to die. Only a few were lucky enough to escape abroad. The Kulaks, who numbered six million people, simply disappeared from the country. During the years 1928–33 all the farming land of Russia, some twenty-five million holdings, was taken over. In the years that followed, agricultural production did increase, but the cost of this in human terms was incalculable.

Meanwhile in the cities Stalin was forging ahead with plans to turn Russia into an industrial country. A series of five-year plans was introduced which were always fulfilled well in advance. The rate of development was extraordinary, but here too it was achieved with little regard to human life and suffering, many workers dying from accidents, exposure and starvation.

It was inevitable that the immense power Stalin wielded would affect his character. He had always been cold and hard and suspicious by nature, but in later years he became obsessed with fears and distrust and devoid of human feelings. He suspected everyone and thought he saw plots and disloyalty on every side. With the rise of Hitler, who had proclaimed his intention of annexing the Ukraine and stamping out Bolshevism, he would have to fight a major war at some time and could not afford to have traitors in his ranks. And so in 1936–37 he initiated a series of political purges. For two years the Russian people were submitted to a terrifying reign of terror. In a series of judicial murders everyone suspected of opposition was brought to public trial, found guilty and condemned to death or a Siberian forced labour camp. Ordinary citizens lived in terror of their lives. Stalin's object was to intimidate the people of Russia to his will. At the same time any remaining freedom of speech was suppressed, vitriolic propaganda was directed against all real and imagined enemies, and history books were rewritten to show that Stalin was always right.

In the 1919 Paris Peace Conference at the end of the First World War delegates had to decide what should happen to the territories wrested from Russia by Germany in the treaty of Brest-Litovsk. Because of the declared intention of Bolshevik leaders to spread communism far and wide there was strong distrust of them and these territories were not restored but divided into a number of new states to form a *cordon sanitaire* separating Russia from the rest of Europe. In this way the country of Poland was resurrected and the Baltic countries of Latvia, Estonia and Lithuania created. With Russia weakened by revolution and civil war the new Polish government thought it could regain territory not allotted to them which had once been part of historic Poland, and rashly mounted an invasion of Russia which was repelled. Bolshevik forces then invaded Poland and caused alarm in Europe when they reached Warsaw. There seemed to be nothing to prevent them from advancing further. However, there then occurred 'the miracle of the Vistula' when the Polish army under its leader, Józef Pilsudski, and with help from the French Marshal Weygand, drove them back. For the time being the advance of communism was stemmed.

In the years that followed, Russia's relations with the rest of Europe have been described as 'suspended war'. Some efforts were made to bring Russia into the community of nations. In 1924 the Bolshevik government was officially recognised by Britain and France; and in 1934 Russia joined the League of Nations, but there was always mistrust and hostility.

Stalin was to show his teeth in 1936 when civil war broke out in Spain. This was between the elected government, an alliance of left-wing parties (liberals, socialists, communists) to be known as Republicans, and rebel forces (mainly monarchist and fascist), known as Nationalists. Stalin should have been ready to help the enemies of fascism and to give support to those revolutionary militias whose aim was to bring communism to Spain; but he seemed less interested in fighting fascism than in suppressing the workers' militias whose members might be communist but not the Stalinist type – Trotskyites perhaps or Anarchists (those who were averse to all forms of central authority and wanted all decisions to be taken by local committees of workers). At his behest these were ruthlessly exterminated. Many foreign volunteers who fought with them including the distinguished English writer George Orwell were lucky to escape with their lives. To him and to others the Spanish Civil War was an eye-opener; it showed that left-wing dictators could be as despotic and ruthless as those of the right.[2]

2 Orwell was to describe his experiences in *Homage to Catalonia* but for a time this could not be published as left-wing English intellectuals like Victor Gollancz and Kingsley Martin in the *New Statesman* could not be shaken in their devotion to Stalin.

CHAPTER TWO

INTERWAR YEARS

Communism not to spread into Western Europe – indifference of working class – support of intelligentsia – determination to admire – enthusiasm of idealistic youth – Cambridge Five – crises of capitalism – Treaty of Versailles – French revenge – reparations unrealistic – collapse of German mark – Great Depression in United States – reckless speculation – effect on Europe – run on pound – Labour government – National Government – drastic cuts – socialism – laissez-faire – free trade – failures of – need for more spending power.

The spread of communism into Western Europe did not get far. There were revolutionary activities of some sort in France and Italy, but these were contained partly by covert action of the American CIA (Central Intelligence Agency) and partly by the influence of the Roman Catholic Church. The British Communist Party, founded in 1920, made little progress, gaining the election of only a handful of representatives either in the House of Commons or in local authorities.

Generally the working class was indifferent but communism had its adherents among the intelligentsia, some of whom were obstinate in their beliefs, not to be put off by the horrors of Stalinism, looking on purges of the innocent by public judicial murders as 'purification' and the extermination of the Kulaks as an essential step in establishing a communist society. Elite visitors to Moscow like Bernard Shaw, H.G. Wells and Julian Huxley were hoodwinked, lapping up everything they were told about communist achievements, of a land of plenty with a joyful, thriving population living off the fat of the land. They would not have had to delve deep to discover the fallacy of this propaganda, but they were determined to admire everything.

Communism was also to arouse enthusiasm among idealistic youth, and nowhere more so than in Trinity College, Cambridge. There for a time in the 1930s it was all the rage with many undergraduates declaring their allegiance to Marxist-Leninism and taking part in animated debates acclaiming the downfall of the bourgeoisie and the dominance of the proletariat. The partisanship of most of these was short-lived; they soon wearied of such subjects as dialectical materialism and determinism and reverted to bourgeois delights – dancing, boating, beagling, flirting.

There were some, however, on whom communism made a lasting impression, in particular a group to become known as the Cambridge Five. They were from middle-class backgrounds except one[3], ex-public school and with leanings towards homosexuality. One of the first of these was Donald Maclean, scholarly and sensitive, son of a Liberal Member of Parliament. Others included Guy Burgess, ex-Etonian, crude, extrovert and intemperate; also was Anthony Blunt, academic, fastidious and to become in time a distinguished

3 John Cairncross, son of a Scottish ironmonger and state educated.

art historian; most notorious of all was Harold Philby (known generally as Kim), pupil of Westminster where he worshipped in the Abbey every day – hard, deceptive and totally ruthless. Most of them had been enrolled into communism and the ranks of the KGB (secret service, once NKVB) by a Soviet agent of great cunning and persuasiveness, Arnold Deutsch, who impressed on them that their contribution to communist revolution would not be writing inflammatory pamphlets or orating on soap boxes at street corners but to keep their beliefs under the counter, blend into the bourgeoisie and lie low, awaiting opportunities; these were to come in abundance with far-reaching consequences.

Although communism was held at bay in Europe during the interwar years, capitalism was to experience its greatest crises, ones which nearly overwhelmed it. There had been one disaster after another. These stemmed mainly from the vindictive Treaty of Versailles which had been formulated in Paris in an emotional and overwrought atmosphere in the immediate aftermath of the First World War. During the war France had suffered massive damage at the hands of the Germans: the north of the country had been occupied for four years, farms laid waste, mines ruined, factories destroyed. The French were determined that this should not happen again, and that Germany should be kept as weak as possible. They therefore demanded the return of Alsace-Lorraine, which was generally agreed, but also annexation of the Rhineland in which there was a large German majority the loss of which would almost certainly have led to another world war. They also demanded huge and unrealistic reparations, far greater than actual war damage. The Germans declared that they could not possibly pay such sums and would only pay that specified in the terms of the Armistice of 1918.

This they were in a position to do as reparations could only be obtained by armed force, and American and British troops were evacuating Europe and France could not enforce them alone. So payment of reparations depended on German cooperation. When this was withheld the French occupied the Ruhr, Germany's industrial heartland, which was followed by a strike of German workers which caused a deadlock. This was to be broken but in 1922–23 there was a collapse of the German monetary system. Suddenly everyone took fright that German paper money was worthless and tried to get rid of it so that the German mark became invalid and a million-mark note could be bought in the streets of London for tuppence. For Germany this was a catastrophe, causing tremendous suffering particularly among the middle classes who saw their life savings disappear overnight. It did, however, have a sobering effect on European and American statesmen in their demands for reparations. It was in no-one's interest that Germany should be in a state of bankruptcy and turmoil.[4]

In 1929 came the Great Depression. This originated in the United States where there was a wave of frantic speculation, investors dazzled by prospects of getting rich quickly and rushing to buy shares, often with borrowed money. This was highly dangerous: as long as the shares continued to rise in price, which at first they did, all was well, but inevitably came the day of reckoning when the grossly inflated values of the shares began to fall and then, as more and more people tried to sell, the fall became an avalanche and many shares became valueless with thousands of people ruined and resorting to suicide or soup kitchens.

The Great Depression in America inevitably had repercussions in Europe where there was great reliance on American loans which suddenly came to an end. The economies of many European countries came under strain,

4 Except perhaps that of Adolf Hitler and the Nazis to whom it provided an opening.

particularly in Britain which was in no condition for such an ordeal. Its economy had been weakened when in 1925, under the auspices of Winston Churchill, the country had returned to the Gold Standard, causing an overvalued pound with a fall in exports and a rise in unemployment. In the late summer of 1930 there came a run on the pound; foreigners rushed to get rid of their English money, and there was the prospect that the pound might become as invalid as the German mark had done a few years before, a nightmare which was to haunt men's minds in the ensuing crisis.

A Labour government (the second) had just taken office, headed as before by Ramsay Macdonald, who was no financial expert and depended on the views of those experts who stated that in order to stop the run on the pound and maintain its value large loans would have to be obtained from abroad and these needed a balanced budget. This would mean drastic economies; severe cuts would have to be made in the salaries of government employees – judges, ministers, teachers, civil servants and the armed services. In addition there would have to be cuts in social services, particularly the large sums spent on unemployment relief. To most members of the Labour government such measures were unthinkable; they would be a denial of everything Labour stood for, and many took the line that, if they had to be done, it would be better to resign and leave it to the Conservatives to do the job. But this was not the view of Ramsay MacDonald. He was not inclined to run away from the crisis. He was convinced that cuts in unemployment relief, though drastic and painful, were the lesser of two evils. Without them the value of the pound might be halved and so too would the living standards of the whole country. And so he tried to persuade his ministers to agree to the course he was taking, but in this he was unsuccessful and everyone expected that he would then resign and make way for a Conservative government; but without consulting his cabinet colleagues he agreed to form a coalition with the Conservatives and Liberals to overcome the crisis. In this he was supported by a few of his ministers; the rest resigned and MacDonald came to be regarded by the main body of Labour as a traitor. The National Government, as the coalition was called, took measures to balance the budget and for a time the run on the pound died down. It had been supposed to last for a limited period until the run on the pound had been overcome but its leaders soon decided that it should be prolonged. In 1931 a general election was held in which it won an overwhelming victory, the Labour Party being almost annihilated. In some form or other the National Government, predominantly Conservatives, was to last until the Second World War.

It was likely that these failures of capitalism would turn people to the opposite camp – that of socialism with its emphasis on working for the common good and antagonism towards private property. Britain's great wealth in the previous century had been based on two main principles – laissez-faire and free trade. Essentially laissez-faire meant individualism and unrestricted freedom in commerce with everyone concentrating on their private interests. Free trade indicated as little interference (known as protection) in trade as possible in the form of tariffs, import duties, export bounties and social legislation to prevent the exploitation of the weak and helpless. It seemed to some that these principles had become out of date, but they should not necessarily be replaced by communism. A new form of capitalism was being evolved, mainly associated with a British economist, John Maynard Keynes. Keynes found great faults with the way the capitalist system operated in the twentieth century. He was convinced that great changes had to be made. 'We have,' he wrote, 'to invent new wisdom for a new age, and in the meantime we must, if we are to do any good, appear unorthodox, troublesome, dangerous, disobedient to them that begat us.' Keynes's solution was a blend of communism and capitalism. It seemed to him that there were two main problems that had to be addressed. The main one was that the law of supply and demand was not working out. Supply was far outstripping demand; with modern methods of production huge quantities of goods could be produced but could not be sold as not enough people had enough money to buy them. The problem therefore was to increase demand by getting more money into more pockets; and the way to do this, according to Keynes, was by large-scale expenditure on public works such as roads, railways and houses. For these projects enough money could not be provided by laissez-faire. Massive credit would have to be used under government control. It followed from this that the usual methods of dealing with financial depressions – rigorous economies, cuts in wages, redundancy of workers – would do more harm than good.

Such measures might bring about lower costs of goods, but at the same time they would create less spending power and less demand for those goods. The cure therefore lay not so much in the reduction of wages as in their increase. Therein lay the answer to unemployment in what came to be called the economics of expansion.

CHAPTER THREE

SECOND WORLD WAR

Invasion of Russia – massive invasion force – Russia overwhelmed – Stalin duped – uneasy alliance with Churchill – advance on Moscow halted, Russia unconquered – Stalingrad – T34 tank – Pearl Harbour – Grand Alliance – end of war – atom bombs on Hiroshima and Nagasaki – death of Roosevelt – Truman, background of – election of Labour government in Britain – Atlantic Charter – inexperience of Truman – Big Three at Potsdam – attitude of Stalin hardened with peace – Britain at end of war – near bankruptcy – loss of prestige – attitude of Roosevelt – communising of Poland – Stalin ruthless – Triumph and Tragedy of Second World War.

On 22 June 1941 at three o'clock in the morning, Hitler declared war on Russia and his armies invaded the country. It was the largest invading force in history: 120 German divisions, eighteen Finnish, sixteen Romanian, three Italian, three Slovakian, over three million men altogether, most highly trained, well organised and equipped with modern arms. The defending Russian forces were fewer in number, inadequately armed and unready for war. This was largely due to Stalin who had been warned by many, including Churchill, that an invasion was impending for which there was plenty of evidence in the massive forces being assembled on the Russian frontier. But these warnings he chose to ignore, looking on them as attempts to draw Russia into war with Germany and thinking that Hitler could be appeased. In an ignominious pact of September 1939 the two arch enemies, one a brigand from a cobbler's shop in Georgia, the other a screaming fanatic from the backstreets of Vienna, each thought they had outwitted the other: Hitler thought it was then safe for him to invade Poland, Stalin that he had gained time for building up Russian forces and reconstructing the army.[5] Both to be fatally undeceived.

Hitler's invasion of Russia came as no surprise to those who had heard his speeches and read his writings of the last ten years. From these it was clear that he had an obsessive hatred of Jews and Bolsheviks whom he wished to stamp out, and had wild ideas of establishing *lebensraum* (living room) in Eastern Europe for the Aryan 'master race' with Slavs and other races in subjection and existing on sufferance. This had always been his main design. Stalin had been duped. To the very end he continued to believe that Hitler could be placated by economic aid and deferring to his wishes; and when Britain and France declared war on Germany in September 1939 he regarded it as 'an imperialist war waged in the interests of the ruling classes', and was more sympathetic to Germany than to the Allies. Even after Russia had been invaded he could not fully accept that it was a proletarian war against fascism.

5 Nearly half of Russian senior generals had been eliminated in Stalin's political purges of 1936–37.

Predictably Russia at first was an easy victim, the German *blitzkrieg* irresistible. Almost at once the Russian air force was grounded, some planes being put out of action, then armoured forces (Panzers) made deep thrusts into Russian territory, leaving vast numbers of infantry surrounded by so-called 'pincer movements', to be mopped up by death or imprisonment.

At the outbreak of hostilities there were many who wondered how Britain and Russia would collaborate as allies. Churchill had been one of the strongest and most outspoken critics of what he called 'the baboonery of Communism', and a strong advocate of aiding the White Russians in the civil war of 1917–21. However, with the German invasion he was uncompromising, pledging all possible aid.[6] But it was not to be an easy alliance. Stalin was aggressive in his demands for aid of all sorts which at that time Britain could ill afford to provide. He was also always insisting that Britain should open up a second front in France at once which would then have been impossible. His attitude was suspicious and he was forever giving the impression that Russia was fighting what was essentially Britain's war, albeit against an enemy in Russian territory. Russia was, however, to bear the brunt of the war against Nazism for the next four years.

After three months it seemed the war was virtually over: German forces had penetrated 300 miles into Russia; in the north Leningrad was under a siege that was to last 900 days; Moscow was within fifteen miles; in the south the Caucasus was not far off; and in the Ukraine the Germans were being welcomed as deliverers by peasants who had been evicted from their farms to make way for collectives. But it was

6 He was quoted as saying: 'I have only one purpose, the destruction of Hitler, and my life is much simplified thereby. If Hitler invaded Hell I would make at least a favourable reference to the Devil in the House of Commons.'

not the end. The final drive on Moscow was delayed on the orders of Hitler who thought the wheatlands of the Ukraine and the industrial areas of the Don and the Dnieper were of greater importance. In the south the Germans gained further victories, but the delay in the advance on Moscow proved fatal. It was nearly successful, near enough for the Russian government to take flight eastwards, but by the time it got underway the Russian winter was setting in. First came heavy rains, turning Russian roads into a morass of mud; and then came frost, twenty degrees of it by mid-November. The Germans were unprepared for this, so confident had Hitler been that the war would be over by then. The German forces had no winter clothing, their vehicles were not starting, their guns not firing, and the batteries of their signalling equipment freezing up. And there was ever more Russian territory to be conquered and apparently unlimited resources of manpower; fresh troops, specially trained and equipped for winter were arriving from Siberia and Mongolia. Hitler, like Napoleon, was discovering that Russia might be an easy country to invade but impossible to conquer. On 5 December the advance on Moscow had to be abandoned.

The halting of the German advance and the counter-attack which followed were miraculous achievements. During the five months since the invasion Russian losses had been colossal: the territory occupied by the Germans contained forty per cent of the Russian population, all their best wheatlands and two-thirds of their coal and heavy industry. No other country could have borne such losses, but the Russian people were undefeated and fighting back, even if it meant only retreating into the vastness of their country, destroying everything as they went. In arms, equipment and military skill the Germans were superior, but in the end it was the courage and endurance of the ordinary Russian soldier which were to prevail.

The retreat from Moscow was a fatal blow to German morale; the first time the German army had been checked and defeated, and there were those among German military commanders who were feeling that they were engaged in an impossible task and looked for a wholesale retreat similar to that of Napoleon's army 130 years before; but Hitler would have none of that. To him victory was essential at all costs.

In 1942 the tide continued to turn in favour of Russia, and this culminated in the battle for Stalingrad, a city of not great strategic importance but of vital prestigious significance. There it was to be the supreme test of the individual fighting qualities of Russian and German soldiers with the former victorious. On 31 January 1943 a German army of 90,000 men surrendered, a victory of decisive consequence. At the same time a war-winning weapon had emerged, the T34 tank. This had been developed in remotest Siberia in darkest secrecy and amid some terrorism.[7] It was to prove superior in armour, speed and fire power to any tank of the Germans or indeed of any country. This was demonstrated forcibly in a mighty tank battle in July 1943 near the city of Kursk in which the German 'Panzers', until then invincible, came off worse. From then on the T34s were at the head of the Russian advances as they drove the Germans out of Russia into Eastern Europe and on to Berlin.

In December 1941 the United States was drawn into the war when Japanese air forces assaulted Pearl Harbour with devastating effect.[8] Hitler then declared war on America. This was one of his greatest errors as it had previously not been certain that America would declare war on Germany. It meant the United States would take the lead in the war

7 One of its chief designers had 'disappeared' in Stalin's purges of 1936–37.

8 Four battleships sunk and four put out of action; altogether eighteen warships were lost or damaged; 350 aircraft were destroyed and total loss of life amounted to nearly 4,000. The Japanese lost twenty-nine aircraft.

in Europe and there was thus formed a Grand Alliance of the United States, Britain and Russia against Germany, Italy and Japan (although Russia did not declare war against Japan until 9 August 1945).

The Grand Alliance did not always run smoothly. There were differences of opinion: some in the United States wanted to give priority to the war against Japan, but Roosevelt insisted that Europe should come first. Stalin strongly urged an immediate opening of a second front in France, but this was impracticable, and Churchill favoured a Mediterranean strategy which was to be adopted with an invasion of French North Africa followed by one of Italy. Stalin was always to be suspicious of Allied intentions and fearful that Russia was bearing the main burden of the war, but he could not deny that Allied actions in North Africa and Italy were holding down some forty German divisions which would have been crucial on the Eastern front.

So long as Germany was undefeated the Grand Alliance held firm, but in 1945 there was a rush of events which created a new situation. On 4 February the Big Three (Stalin, Roosevelt and Churchill) met in Yalta in the Crimea where the atmosphere was reasonably concordant. Churchill was to pay Stalin a genial compliment: 'I walk through this world with greater courage and hope when I find myself in a relationship of friendship and industry with this great man.' To this Stalin replied equally warmly, describing Churchill as 'the most courageous of all prime ministers in the world, embodying political experience with military leadership who when all Europe was ready to fall flat before Hitler said that Britain would stand and fight alone against Germany even without any allies.' This bonhomie was not to last long. It became evident that the Grand Alliance was only an intermission in the struggle between capitalism and communism. There were deep-rooted differences: the power of democracies depended on votes of the people, that of communism on repression and terrorism. The war aims of the Western Allies had been set out in the first meeting of Churchill and Roosevelt in August 1941 in the Atlantic Charter which stated unequivocally the right of people to choose their own form of government and to live free from fear and want. Stalin was to pay lip service to this but only when it suited him.

The first sign of a change of heart came on 12 April 1945 with the death of President Roosevelt, to be succeeded by Harry Truman, almost unknown and inexperienced and inevitably at something of a loss. Nine days later Russian forces entered Berlin and with the end of the war in sight came a hardening in the attitude of Stalin – more demanding and rigid. On 30 April Hitler committed suicide and on 8 May the war in Europe came to an end. The war with Japan continued for three months but on 10 August after atomic bombs had been dropped on Hiroshima and Nagasaki the Japanese surrendered and open warfare came to an end. By then a general election had been held in Britain and the Conservative Party of Winston Churchill had been overwhelmed by the Labour Party led by Clement Attlee who became prime minister on 26 July.

Harry Truman, the new president of the United States and the most powerful man in the world, seemed to be a man of no great distinction. He had been born and brought up on a farm in Missouri and had served in the army during the First World War, attaining the rank of captain. On demobilisation he took to the trade of haberdashery and was to rise rapidly in the hierarchy of Missouri, becoming a judge, although apparently without judicial functions.

In 1935 he was elected to the US Senate as a member of the Democratic Party in which at first he made no great name for himself, and when he was chosen by Roosevelt to be his running mate as vice president in the 1944 election it caused surprise. It seemed that Roosevelt was seeking someone of minor repute who could be ignored and kept in the background. He was to hold that office, however, for only eleven weeks before on the death of Roosevelt he was propelled into becoming president. He had had little experience of politics at national level and none at all internationally. The responsibilities awaiting him were awesome: the war against Germany had to be finished off, and victory over Japan was unsettled. In a few months' time the haberdasher from Missouri was due to attend a conference of the Big Three at Potsdam alongside Winston Churchill and Josef Stalin. While he was there he was to be informed of the existence of atom bombs ready to be dropped on Japan, and it was up to him to decide whether this was to be done. He was in little doubt about it. Like nearly all other war leaders he was convinced that, horrific as atomic weapons were, the use of them would cause fewer human casualties, especially among the Japanese, than the invasion of the country by conventional forces. But it was a terrible decision to have to take, causing as it did some 78,000 deaths – no man before or since has brought death to so many civilians at one stroke.

The situation of Britain at the end of the war was dismal. It had been the first country to declare war on Nazism and on its own initiative, not waiting until it had been attacked, as with Russia and America. During the war the country had suffered devastating hardships – bombed, blitzed, nearly starved out, suffering humiliating defeats as well as heroic victories. Total war deaths were estimated at 357,000 (including 42,000 civilians), 130,000 homes had been destroyed and at one time fifty ships a month were being sunk in the Atlantic alone.

The wealth of the country in the form of foreign investments had long since been expended and its economy was maintained by instalments of Lend-Lease from America.

When these were suddenly withdrawn at the end of the war the country was left stranded on the verge of bankruptcy. The Labour government was committed to the introduction of a welfare state (including a National Health Service) which, however beneficial, was hardly affordable. It was also to embark on plans for the nationalisation of coal mines, railways and iron and steel. At the same time the country's overseas responsibilities were as heavy as ever – bearing its share in financing a devastated Europe, maintaining order in a disaffected India, and keeping the peace between Jew and Arab in Palestine. This meant that a huge loan had to be obtained from America but this was only obtainable on strictly commercial terms. Britain's desperate economic situation meant the loss of prestige worldwide. It could no longer carry the same weight in the council of nations.

This became conspicuous in the last days of Roosevelt. In his prime he had worked wonders for which Britain was deeply indebted to him but in old age a change had come over him. His physical condition had declined and his judgement impaired. He was obsessed by the need for an immediate victory over Japan and was convinced that Russian aid was necessary for this, it being before the full development of atom bombs. In his latter days he had gone out of his way to be conciliatory towards Stalin and had not taken a firm stand with Churchill in resisting Stalin's domination of Eastern Europe. He had been too acquiescent and this had facilitated Stalin's imposition of communist despotisms on East European countries. At this time too he was making clear his aversion to the British Empire, looking on it as outdated and wrongful and asserting that the United States was not waging war to preserve it. He was strongly critical of colonialism with one race subjecting another, but in this he was not altogether objective. American history had not been free of it. In pursuit of Manifest Destiny (ordained by God to control the whole of the North American continent) the American government had annexed nearly all of southern California (about 500,000 square miles), nearly half the terrain of the Mexican Republic. Also at the end of the war with Spain in 1898 the United States annexed for a time the Philippine islands in the Pacific. Roosevelt might also have borne in mind that slavery in the British Empire was abolished in 1833 and did not come to a complete end in America until 1865; and that in his own time Afro-Americans did not have the same freedom and rights as European Americans.

With the coming of peace the main controversy concerned Poland, an issue on which both Stalin and Churchill had strong opposing views. To Churchill it was on Poland's behalf that Britain had gone to war disinterestedly in 1939. It was not possible to withstand the occupation of the country by Germany and Russia, but since then many Poles (some 150,000) had sought refuge in the West and were fighting alongside Allied forces in North Africa and Italy, and a Polish government in exile had been set up in London which was in contact with an underground movement in Warsaw. Towards them Churchill felt a strong bond but Stalin had a different view. To him Poland was the gateway of German armies into Russia which had occurred several times in history, and he was determined that Poland should be communised and become a vassal state of Russia. At the Yalta Conference he had undertaken that there would be 'free and unfettered elections' in the country with universal suffrage and independent candidature, but this was a promise he was not to keep. At his instigation a Polish government, known as that of Lublin, was instituted under Russian domination. The relationship between London and Lublin Poles became deeply hostile. Lublin had full Russian support and Stalin had only one way of overcoming opposition – to eliminate it. In Katyn in 1942 there were found mass graves of some

4,000 Polish officers who had been shot in cold blood on Stalin's orders, as was later discovered. There were also some 11,000 others who had 'disappeared'. In 1944 he had been even more dastardly when the Russian army had approached Warsaw and he ordered them to halt while the Polish underground which had risen in support on orders from London was massacred by the German Gestapo. And so in the end there was a Polish government set up in the words of Marshal Tito of Yugoslavia 'at the points of Russian bayonets'.

Churchill realised that communism could not be resisted. The Second World War had not, as hoped, been a victory for democracy. He was to give the title of his memoirs *Triumph and Tragedy*.

CHAPTER FOUR

POST WAR 1945–49

Truman at Potsdam and in office – Churchill oratory – Truman and Stalin – war crimes – Soviet expansion – reparations – Greece and Turkey – new era – Truman Doctrine – Marshall Aid – Soviet ban – revival of West Germany – a dominant force – Cominform – Warsaw Pact – German Democratic Republic – Berlin – Allied zones – at Russia's mercy – Berlin blockade – Berlin Airlift – Western mistrust – pattern of Communist domination – in Poland, Hungary, Romania, Bulgaria, Albania, Czechoslovakia – Yugoslavia – NATO – German Federal Republic – European Coal and Steel Community – Britain absent – British difficulties – Treaty of Rome – Common Market – Ernest Bevin – Clement Attlee.

At the meeting of the Big Three, Truman, not unduly overawed, was to give off-the-cuff descriptions of those he met there. Like Roosevelt he was to be beguiled by Stalin who could put on a civilised face when it suited him. 'I can deal with

Stalin,' he said. 'He is honest and smart as hell.' By Churchill he was less impressed: 'Most charming and very pleasant but too much soft soap about loving America and what a great country it is and how much he loved Roosevelt and intended to love me.' Of the Labour Prime Minister, Clement Attlee, when he arrived on the scene to take Churchill's place he was inclined to be dismissive. Like many others he underestimated him. He was later to have different views.

The multifarious problems confronting him were not eased by his standing in America where he was regarded by many as an inadequate makeshift president, not up to the job and with little hope in the impending presidential election in 1948. But he was not to be put off. He spared himself no pains and was determined to 'do his damnedest', and on his desk were the words enframed: 'the buck stops here.' In these homely circumstances his achievements were to be momentous. Churchill was to say of him: 'You, more than any other man, have saved Western civilisation.'

Churchill, although out of office, was not to be silent. He spoke out trenchantly, and there was no voice more widely heeded. Soon after his election defeat he was to speak of Europe in despondent terms:

> *What is Europe now? It is a rubble heap, a charnel house, a breeding ground of pestilence and hate... Is there then to be no respite? Has Europe's mission come to an end? Has she nothing to give the world but the contagion of the Black Death? Are her people to go on harrying and tormenting one another by war and vengeance until all that invests human life with dignity and comfort has been obliterated? Are we all through our poverty and our quarrels for ever to be a burden and danger to the rest of the world?*

These words were to ring round universally and later, on 5 March 1946, they were to ring even more clearly in an historic speech in Fulton, Missouri:

> *From Stettin in the Baltic to Trieste in the Adriatic an iron curtain has descended across the Continent. From what I have seen of our Russian friends and allies during the war I am convinced there is nothing they admire so much as strength and there is nothing for which they have less respect than for military weakness.*

Truman was in the audience during the address and was impressed by it, but he had not yet cast off the mantle of Roosevelt and was still engaged in coming to terms with Stalin. For a short time after the war it had seemed that it might be possible for communism and capitalism to coexist reasonably peacefully. There had been, in the main, agreement about the future of Germany; the zones of the occupying powers (America, Russia, Britain and France) had been settled and a control commission set up for the whole country. The Allies were agreed on keeping Germany weak and demilitarised and its industrial capacity reduced so that it would not again be a threat to Europe. It was also agreed that the principal Nazi leaders should be brought to trial for the waging of aggressive war[9] and crimes against humanity – death camps, shooting prisoners of war, imposition of forced labour. There was some hesitation about putting on trial and executing leaders of a defeated country, but it was felt that the crimes of the Nazis had been so horrendous that they called for unique retribution. And so some were condemned to be hanged and some to long terms of imprisonment.

9 On this score Russian conscience might be uneasy in view of their invasion of Poland and Finland in 1939, but these events were glossed over.

Winston Churchill, Franklin D. Roosevelt and Josef Stalin at the Yalta Conference, February 1945.

British Prime Minister Clement Attlee, President Harry Truman and Josef Stalin at the Potsdam Conference, July 1945.

At first in disputes between communism and capitalism the Russians usually prevailed. Under the plea that they had to have maximum security from another German invasion they had taken possession of vast tracts of territory in Poland, Romania and East Germany and moved into the Baltic states of Estonia, Latvia and Lithuania and regained lands from Japan in the Far East. Altogether some twenty-four million people had been added to the Soviet Union, and further claims were pending in Iran, Turkey and Finland. At the same time Russian armies were stationed in Eastern Europe to bring their influence to bear on the political stance of governments there.

The first serious conflict between Russia and the Western Allies arose over the reparations to be paid by Germany. The Russians insisted that these should be as large as possible, and quantities of industrial plant and machinery were being transported across Europe. It was thought by many that this was justifiable in view of the massive losses of Russia during the war, but it was considered that in return Russia should send food from the East to prevent starvation, and this they were not doing. As a result the Western Allies were having to buy food from abroad which Britain in particular could ill afford. This meant in effect that the West was subsidising Russian reparations, and on 3 May 1946 the Americans announced that for the time being no more reparations would be sent. This marked a turning point in East-West relations intensifying the so-called Cold War, described as 'all hostilities short of general war'.

By early 1947 Truman had become disillusioned about Soviet communism, and when in February the British government gave notice that it was no longer able to provide armed support to Greece and Turkey in combating communist insurgents, he decided at once to send American forces in their place. This was a landmark – the first time the United States army would be taking arms against the forces of communism. It was the beginning of an era. There was opposition in the Senate from some who spoke up for 'a fortress America free from overseas obligations', but the move was approved, and this marked the end of American isolationism. From then the United States would not be confined to its own boundaries but would be assuming active roles in world affairs. At the same time Truman enunciated what came to be known as *The Truman Doctrine*, pledging American support for 'people who are resisting attempted subjugation by armed minorities or outside pressures, and assistance for free people to work out their own destinies in their own way'.

This declaration was to be followed by more positive action. In January 1947 General George Marshall had been appointed by Truman as Secretary of State. A man of exceptional ability and integrity, he had been throughout the Second World War chief of general staff of the American army and in effect its overall commander-in-chief. Few were held in such esteem. At the end of the war he was preparing to go into retirement when he was called on by Truman to go to China to give advice and backbone to President Chiang Kai-shek and to bring some sort of order into his chaotic army. This had proved an impossible task, partly due to the incapacity of Chiang and partly to the vital powers of the communist leader Mao Tse-Tung who in time was to overcome all of China. A quiet, unassuming man, Marshall was to become one of America's most creative Secretaries of State, determined that Europe was to be rescued from its parlous condition. Truman let him have a free hand and it was given to him to lay down the future of the United States and Europe.

On 5 June 1947 at Harvard University he outlined a plan for the reconstruction of Europe. The low morale and tottering

Harry S. Truman. Haberdasher from Missouri and
33rd President of the United States 1945–1952.

economies of European countries were to be boosted by a massive injection of US dollars which would enable them to restore their industries and provide employment and a fair standard of living for their people. In making this offer Marshall made it clear that America was not seeking to interfere in the governments of European countries. Marshall Aid, as it came to be known, was not directed against any country or doctrine but against poverty, hunger, desperation and chaos. For that reason it was open to all European countries including Eastern Europe, even Russia, but this was refused by Stalin who looked on it as an encroachment into the domestic affairs of other countries. Cooperation with America was something he could not tolerate; in order to maintain his despotic powers at home he needed a foreign enemy with which to intimidate the Russian people. American imperialism had to be held up as a threat to the world.

Marshall Aid was to prove a timely rescue of Western European countries. Their economies were revived and a fresh, more optimistic spirit aroused. This was particularly the case with West Germany whose economy was transformed so that it became a dominant force, no longer a defeated enemy but a vital ally. Of course Stalin took alarm at this and drew the satellite states of East Europe more closely together, first in 1947 with the Cominform (Communist Information Bureau) to coordinate activities in Europe, and then in 1955 into a closer union similar to NATO by which they would come to one another's assistance if under attack, known as the Warsaw Pact. The Russian zone of East Germany was converted into the German Democratic Republic as an independent state with the purpose of 'socialist construction'. And Stalin was also always looking for ways of weakening the Western Alliance, and its most vulnerable point had to be Berlin.

By an agreement made in wartime, Britain, America and France had been allocated zones in Berlin. The position of these was precarious – tiny islands over a hundred miles inside the main Russian zone, dependent on the Russians for supply of electricity and road and rail links with Western Europe. They seemed to lie at Russia's mercy. Even so the Russians proceeded at first with caution, but at the end of March 1948 they started to interfere with land traffic to West Berlin and to close down roads and railways, making the excuse that repairs were necessary. By the end of June all land communications were cut off completely.

To the Western powers it seemed at first that there were two possible courses of action: they could submit to being squeezed out of Berlin or they could blast their way through. The first would mean a calamitous humiliation, the second would mean open war. But then a third possibility emerged – to keep Berlin supplied with all essentials by air. This was a daunting prospect: it would involve flying in every day thousands of tons of food and fuel. On examination, however, the scheme seemed feasible, and on 25 June 1948 the Berlin Airlift began.

This was to be an amazing achievement. After six months there was an average of 552 flights a day,[10] and by then 700,000 tons of food, fuel and other supplies had been landed. A few months later on 16 April 1949 a record 1,400 flights were made, carrying some 1,300 tons, so that more goods were then coming into the city than before the blockade. This mighty show of strength had a great effect on both the Russians and the inhabitants of West Berlin. Throughout the bitterly cold winter West Berliners were ready to accept any hardship rather than be absorbed into the Russian sector. For their part the Russians had a great sense of failure; they were not going to be able to force the Western powers out of Berlin; it had been clearly

10 The proportion was about two-thirds American and one third British.

demonstrated that they were not there on sufferance. On 12 May 1949 the blockade was lifted.

The Berlin Airlift enhanced the division of Europe between East and West. The Western democracies became ever more suspicious of Stalin's intentions. Why did he maintain such a large standing army? So much larger than was necessary for the defence of Russia. Where would he strike next?

His domination of Eastern Europe had become complete. The pattern by which he gained control of East European administrations was usually similar. First there would be a coalition in which the communists shared power with other parties, but ensured that they held key posts, notably in the police and armed forces. Then in time the communists would discredit the others and oust them. Some might fight back, but there was always the spectre of the Russian army ready to intervene. In this way, as has been seen in Poland, the government was communised.

The same happened in Hungary where in an election in 1945 the Smallholders Party won a clear majority but was not allowed by Stalin to form a government on their own and was to give way to a United Workers' Party under Matyas Rákosi, a hardened communist of Jewish origins. During the war Romania had fought on the side of the Russians for which King Michael had been awarded the Order of Victory; but at the end of 1947 he was dethroned to make way for a People's Republic, later changed to a Socialist Republic. In Bulgaria the monarchy was abolished in September 1946 and a People's Republic established under Georgi Dimitrov, a long-standing communist if not always a compliant one. In Albania the Russians set up a strict Stalinist dictatorship under Enver Hoxha who was to hold on through the various tergiversations of communism until his death in 1985. The state that resisted Russian rule the longest was

Czechoslovakia, where in an election in 1946 communists won only 114 seats out of 300. A coalition ensued and gradually communists replaced members of other parties. In 1948 a new administration was installed, headed by Klement Gottwald. Jan Masaryk, Czech patriot of international renown and leading anti-communist, was a member but on 10 March he died in mysterious circumstances.[11] The only state to withstand Russia permanently was Yugoslavia where at the end of the war Josip Broz (son of a blacksmith, and long-serving communist known as Marshal Tito) had seized power without Russian aid and was to become an independent voice which was not to be tolerated by Stalin who tried to dislodge him. 'I will shake my little finger and there will be no more Tito,' he declared. But he was to survive, a loose cannon in the Soviet bloc until his death in 1980.

Under the auspices of America, and General Marshall in particular, the states of Western Europe were drawing closer together and seeing the need for their common defence. In a speech in 1947, Churchill had declared that Europe had to unite. 'Old rivalries and barriers,' he declared, 'must be eliminated. The people of Europe must be persuaded to join forces.' Moreover it was essential to start immediately when the Continent was in ruins. This was 'a supreme opportunity'. On 4 April 1949 the North Atlantic Pact was signed by the United States, Britain, France, Benelux (Belgium, Holland and Luxemburg), Italy, Portugal, Iceland, Denmark, Norway and Canada. This instituted a North Atlantic Treaty Organisation (to be known as NATO) which was to provide for joint defence, it being affirmed that an attack against one of these countries was to be taken as an attack on all of them. At the same time the American, British and French zones of

11 He fell from a window of the Foreign Office. It has never been established whether this was suicide or murder.

Germany were united to form the German Federal Republic with the capital at Bonn.

Some had fears that Marshall Aid might lead to a rapid recovery of Germany which would become again a menace to the rest of Europe; but Robert Schuman of France maintained that this danger could be avoided if the main industries of Europe (coal, steel, iron) could be merged. This led in 1951 to the Treaty of Paris which established the European Coal and Steel Community (ECSC), to be absorbed in 1957 by the Treaty of Rome which set up the European Economic Community (EEC) with closer economic ties including free movement for workers, capital and goods between member states. The signatories to this treaty were France, West Germany, Italy and Benelux. The conspicuous absentee was Britain which could have joined but stayed out. The post-war Labour government had always been hesitant. It was ready to work closely with other countries in such matters as finance and defence, but was unwilling to give up any of Britain's sovereign powers to a supra-national body in which Britain was only one of several with the power to overrule governments concerning their own affairs. Churchill had said that surrender of national sovereignty was the crux of European unity and without it no union could have any true meaning; but when he became prime minister again in 1951 he held back. There were serious difficulties in Britain joining the Common Market: there were strong ties with the Commonwealth with trading arrangements which would have to be abandoned, and Britain's so-called 'special relationship' with the United States would be diminished. There was as well a feeling of isolation and prejudice against foreigners and being subject to their decisions. And so for the time being Britain stayed out.

Britain's part in European unity should not be underestimated. The country had had a vital role in the launching of the Marshall Plan and the institution of NATO.

This was mainly the work of Ernest Bevin, Labour foreign secretary and one of the great holders of that office. He was an unconventional diplomat; from lowly origins, an orphan at the age of eight who had started life as a farm labourer, then became a docker, and in due course the most powerful trade unionist in the country when he managed to unite nearly fifty unions into the Transport and General Workers' Union, the largest in the world. During the Second World War he had served in Churchill's government as minister of labour, responsible for organising the nation's work forces. After the war he was a mainstay of the Labour government, a moderate socialist[12] and staunch opponent of left-wing ideologues. In meetings of foreign ministers he was an incongruous figure – rugged and blunt and lacking the finesse of professional diplomats, but he was almost invariably to inspire respect and affection. Some expected that he might be more inclined towards communist Russia than to capitalist America but this was not so: he became strongly averse to communism and a strong upholder of freedom and democracy.

He worked in close conjunction with the Labour Prime Minister, Clement Attlee, a man of a different sort – ex-public school, army officer and in middle age a member of the Labour Party and mayor of Stepney in London's East End where he was deeply shocked by the poverty of the people. He became leader of the Labour Party in 1935 and in Churchill's wartime coalition he was deputy prime minister. He was a marked contrast to Churchill – no orator, plain spoken, unpretentious, businesslike and brisk. In Labour's sweeping victory in the general election of 1945 he was a sobering influence, no wild revolutionary, although during his six years as prime minister he achieved much including

12 Labour socialism was indeed far removed from Russian Marxism. Malcolm Muggeridge described it as having as much appeal to Stalin as ginger beer to a congenital drunkard.

Ernest Bevin. Trade unionist, Labour foreign secretary and strong opponent of communism at the Council of Europe, 1949.

the nationalisation of coal mines and railways, the National Health Service and the independence of India – more than any other peacetime prime minister until the arrival of Mrs Thatcher. He was also to give invaluable support and some guidance to President Truman.

Berlin Airlift. West Berliners look on as plane lands with part of 700,000 tons of food fuel and other supplies brought in, 1948.

CHAPTER FIVE

SUBTERFUGE

Russians with upper hand – beginning of Cold War – decline of MI5 and MI6 – Enigma – Cambridge Five during war – breakdown of Donald Maclean – to Moscow with Guy Burgess – missing diplomats – Philby under suspicion – investigated – acquitted – Macmillan in House of Commons – Philby reinstated – in Beirut – newspaper correspondent – back with KGB – Blake affair – Philby uncovered – Flora Solomon – escape of Philby – reaction in UK and USA – Philby in Moscow – apologia – Blunt and Cairncross redeemed – Rosenberg and Hiss in USA.

While statesmen were negotiating and orating in public, a war was being waged between intelligence forces underground. A few days after the surrender of Germany a Russian cipher clerk, Igor Gouzenko, defected in Canada with some 109 confidential documents which revealed widespread Soviet espionage. This was the beginning of what was to become known as the Cold War.

In this at first the Russians were to have the upper hand. They had considerable advantages. They were fielding many more personnel all over the world, more than a million altogether, some officially in embassies with diplomatic status and many more at large as independent 'illegals' finding out what they could and stirring up trouble wherever it might arise. At that time British intelligence forces were not in good order.

In the war with Germany they had had notable successes: German spies landed by parachute or submarine or smuggled in as refugees had been rounded up and then subjected to what was known as 'double cross' by which they were turned into double agents sending disinformation to Germany. A major breakthrough had been 'Enigma', a device which decrypted German secret messages, laying bare their war plans, which was to prove a war winner. Since the war ended British intelligences (MI5 on the home front and MI6 abroad) had declined: talented university dons reverted to academic life and other bright lights to peacetime occupations, and their replacements were a mixed bag, some hardly up to the job.[13]

A dangerous situation was to arise when there was a rift between the two services. MI6 members saw themselves as an elite autonomous body which went its own way without interference from others, notably not from MI5 whom they regarded with some disdain as being both militarily and socially inferior.[14] As will be seen, this difference was to become acute on a matter of serious importance.

Russian preponderance in espionage was also due to a number of communist sympathisers including British

13 MI5 was once described by Lord Justice Birkett as 'illiberal, disorganised and incompetent', and accused by a government minister of 'pathological stupidities'.

14 A similar state of affairs was to occur in other countries: in America between the CIA (Central Intelligence Agency) and the FBI (Federal Bureau of Investigation) and in Russia between the KGB (secret service) and GRU (military intelligence).

scientists of international renown. In 1946 the physicist Alan Nunn May, who had been engaged in the Manhattan Project developing the atom bomb, was compelled to confess that he had been sending secret information to the Russians. For this he was sentenced to ten years' imprisonment of which he served six and a half.

A more calamitous offender was Klaus Fuchs, a Jewish refugee from Nazi Germany and brilliant scientist, who was also engaged on the Manhattan Project. He was to make a full confession in 1949 that he had betrayed vital information which, some believed, enabled the Russians to have an atomic bomb years earlier than might have been. For this he was sentenced to fourteen years in prison of which he was to serve nine. Both he and May were unrepentant for what they had done, maintaining that in the confrontation between two great superpowers it was mortally dangerous for one side only to have such massive means of destruction and that world peace depended on both of them possessing them.

The Russians were also to have formidable assistance from the so-called Cambridge Five. After being enrolled in the KGB in Cambridge in the 1930s they had taken part in the war against Nazi Germany, and in spite of their communist associations had obtained high-ranking posts – Burgess and Maclean in the Foreign Office, Cairncross as private secretary to a cabinet minister, Blunt in MI5 and Philby in MI6. With the coming of peace they had to decide whether their loyalty lay with capitalist America or communist Russia, and they were all to opt for the latter. For some time they operated successfully, passing on all that came their way to their controllers and thence to Moscow; but they lived on a knife edge, liable to be unmasked and at times under great strain.

The first to crack was Donald Maclean. He had worked diligently and efficiently in the Foreign Office and come in for rapid promotion. In 1944 he was appointed first secretary in the British Embassy in Washington where he had access to much secret information. He was to be in Washington for four years and for most of that time he was well respected and above suspicion. But his behaviour became erratic – often drunk and disorderly and *in vino veritas* (truth in wine) he became highly indiscreet, joking about his communist past and how he was 'working for Uncle Joe' (Stalin). Strangely, these outbursts were treated light-heartedly, regarded as no more than frivolous peccadilloes. Few doubted his loyalty. In 1948 he was appointed to a senior post as counsellor and head of chancery in the British Embassy in Cairo, then seething with espionage of all sorts.

His behaviour there was to become scandalous (consorting with rough characters from off the street), but his British employers were still inclined to ignore such escapades. But then American code breakers (known as Venona) discovered that almost for certain he was a double agent. At first British intelligence was to take no immediate action, hoping to catch him *in flagrante delicto* (red-handed), but he was brought back to England and kept under surveillance. His Russian controller, however, became more seriously alarmed, fearing that in his cups he would spill the beans over his spying activities. He therefore ordered him in 1951 to leave the country and take refuge behind the Iron Curtain, and to see him on his way his colleague in espionage, Guy Burgess, was to accompany him.

Guy Burgess was an irregular spy, a joker in the pack – boisterous, outgoing and loose-living; an avowed and rampant homosexual liable to arrest and imprisonment when at that time such practices were illegal. He was rarely out of trouble but was usually extricated by his charm and good humour; but he overstepped the mark. He had to be sent home in disgrace from a post in America after clashes with the law, when his Russian controller decided that he was too much of a loose cannon and had to be silenced, which could be achieved by ordering him with Maclean to Moscow. Burgess was to do what he was told, little knowing what he was in for. He expected a short mission and that he would soon be back, up to his old tricks, only to find that it was a life sentence, trapped in Moscow, unable to return to England without being arraigned for treason. He and Maclean were not to be made public in Moscow for five years, during much of which time they were headline news.

Seldom has there been such a furore as that over 'the missing diplomats'. They were to be the subject of conversation and speculation in all walks of life, the press offering huge rewards for the slightest information about them. In Moscow at the heart of it all were two wan, dispirited creatures trying to conform to an alien way of life. Maclean made some attempt to adapt, finding useful occupations, but Burgess remained always restless and bored. The Russians tried to cheer him up with a reasonably comfortable apartment along with a consenting adult, but he was always to long for a free bourgeois existence. He died in 1968 at the age of fifty-eight.

Directly after the disappearance of Burgess and Maclean, Philby was to come under dark suspicion. Of all the spies and double agents in the history of espionage few have been so potent and so ruthless as Harold Adrian Russell Philby (generally known as Kim). No other Englishman has wrought such damage to his country. For nearly thirty years on and off he lived a double life as a highly placed British intelligence officer and at the same time an agent of the Russian secret police (KGB, previously NKVB). During that time he is reputed to have undermined as many as twenty-five major operations and caused the deaths of many hundreds of anti-communist activists. For these he felt no compunction, saying pitilessly that 'war is war' and they had to go. For all his life he was constantly in danger, liable to be unmasked by the turn of events and brought to justice; but as well as having great courage he was also a supreme actor. It is incredible for how long he was able to deceive close friends, colleagues and family including mother, three wives and five children. As one wife was to say of him ruefully: 'No one ever really knows another human being.'

In the Second World War he contrived at an early stage to be taken into military intelligence (MI6) and was to prove a highly efficient and hard-working officer who was to have rapid promotion. He was respected and fully trusted by his colleagues, none having any idea that he was secretly plotting their downfall. In 1949 he was sent to the British Embassy in Washington as chief of MI6 there, which brought him into close contact with the CIA (Central Intelligence Agency) with access to numerous secret documents to be passed on to Moscow.

Philby's run of success came to an abrupt end with the defection of Burgess and Maclean for he had made a fatal mistake of befriending Burgess and allowing him to lodge in the basement of his Washington residence. Following the departure of the two diplomats there was a widespread belief that there was a third man behind the scenes who had warned them and engineered their escape; and Philby was a prime suspect. This was to cause a major division of opinion. In England MI5 was almost certain that he was a double agent but this was hotly denied by MI6 who resented such a slur on one of their number. Action, however, had to be taken as in America the FBI (Federal Bureau of Investigation) under J. Edgar Hoover was convinced of his guilt and was urging immediate action; but MI6 was insistent that this had to be gentlemanly and respectable. There should be nothing resembling Soviet ways.

These had been seen blatantly in 1944 when Konstantin Volkov, a consular official in Istanbul, had attempted to defect – bringing with him a list of Soviet agents in Britain and Turkey with other relevant details. But the KGB was to get wind of this and acted promptly. Hit men were sent in to abduct Volkov and his wife and managed to take them back to Moscow for the torture chamber and execution.

There was to be nothing like this in the case of Philby who was to be 'invited', not ordered, to come to England to help in enquiries and be treated as an officer and a gentleman and then, if necessary, be taken to court for trial by jury. MI5 knew that for this there was not at present adequate evidence, only circumstantial, nothing positive. What was needed was a confession and this they tried to extract from him by various means – some conciliatory, some blustering, some cunning. But Philby was aware of what they wanted and was determined they should not have it, nor did they. All attempts were resisted and Philby had to be declared innocent. But he had to leave MI6; he was too widely mistrusted. And so he was out in the cold on his own, but this was not to be for long.

In MI6 he still had friends and supporters who were convinced of his innocence. One of these in particular, Nicholas Elliott, son of the provost of Eton, found it impossible to believe that Philby was a spy and was determined to show that the charges against him were false and no more than 'unsubstantiated conjecture'. He was able to make contact with Harold Macmillan, the foreign secretary, and persuaded him that Philby was guiltless so that Macmillan made a statement in the House of Commons on 7 November 1955 in which he declared plainly: 'I have no reason to conclude that Mr Philby has at any time betrayed the interests of this country or to identify him with the so-called "third man" if, indeed, there was one.' This seemed final and definitive, and Philby was to give an interview to the press, suave and imperturbable, in which he dismissed out of hand any idea that he had been a communist let alone a Russian spy.

Elliott had achieved much but he was not to be satisfied: he wanted to see Philby not only vindicated but reinstated into MI6, and in this he had some success, getting him appointed as a special agent in Beirut as well as newspaper correspondent for *The Observer* and *Economist*.

Beirut at that time was a centre of espionage, political intrigue and undercover operations of all sorts; it was also in the midst of a Lebanese civil war. For the seven years that Philby was to be there he became involved in most of these activities. At an early stage he was approached by an agent of the KGB to resume his espionage on their behalf, and this he agreed to do. There was no need for this. He could have bowed out, but the temptation was too great: spying was in his blood as too was the wielding of secret power. From then on he was to be in regular communication with a Russian case officer, reporting whatever he had been able to pick up which was not always of much significance, but he kept in contact for the sake of it and in case of emergencies.

At first everything went well for him; he dashed off his journalism easily and quickly, did not put himself out unduly in espionage and was happily married (for the third time) to an attractive and high-spirited American lady; and with MI6 in England he was still trusted.

This tranquil period, however, was not to last. Storm clouds were gathering and Nemesis[15] was approaching. He was to be hard hit by certain events. The death of his father, the explorer St John Philby, in 1960 affected him unexpectedly deeply. Their relationship had not been warm, rather in the nature of love-hate, but they did have much in common –

15 Goddess of Vengeance and Retribution.

both intractable contrarians, obdurately opinionated and not to be put off course by public opinion, Kim by devotion to communism and St John to Arabism.[16]

Philby was also greatly shaken by the fantastic career of George Blake, once George Behar of Dutch-Jewish-Egyptian descent. Blake was incarcerated for a time by the Nazis, then after being taken into MI6, he was to be imprisoned for three years in North Korea. There he was converted into communism and on his return to England became a double agent in MI6 and the KGB. In 1960 MI6 sent him to Beirut for a course in Arabic at a special languages school, but while there he was unmasked as a traitor by the evidence of a Russian defector Anatoly Golitsyn. Inveigled back to England he was induced into making a full confession, hoping thereby for clemency which he was not to have. After trial at the Old Bailey in 1961 he was sentenced to forty-two years' imprisonment, then the longest ever imposed. That was not, however, the end of the story. In 1966 he was abducted from Wormwood Scrubs by helicopter, carried out by a sympathetic group, and whisked off to Moscow where he spent the rest of his life in comparative repose.

The severity of Blake's sentence came as a profound shock to Philby who realised more clearly than ever how great was the danger in which he existed. At last his nerve began to crack and he resorted more and more to alcohol. No longer as composed and self-confident as he had once been he became convinced that his downfall was near at hand, as it was. This happened partly as a result of revelations of the Soviet defector Anatoly Golitsyn which mentioned a Cambridge spy-ring in which no names were given but those concerned were identifiable. At the same time MI6 found the

16 As shown when at the age of forty-five he converted to Islam and at sixty taking as his second wife a slave girl of sixteen presented to him by Ibn Saud, first monarch of Saudi Arabia.

hardcore evidence they had long been seeking that Philby had once been an active communist agent in England.

This came from an improbable source. Flora Solomon was a lady of ability and force of character. Born in Russia in 1895, into a well-to-do Jewish family, she escaped during the Bolshevik revolution to England where she married a temporary brigadier-general. In the 1950s she became a friend of Kim Philby who tried unsuccessfully to persuade her to become a member of the Communist Party to which he belonged. In the following years she was to keep quiet about this, thinking, when Philby was in trouble, that he was being smeared unjustly and she was to occupy herself assiduously as a highly effective welfare officer in Marks and Spencer. She was, however, to become incensed by some of Philby's articles from Beirut which seemed to her anti-Israel in tone, while she was a passionate Zionist. And so she told of her involvement with Philby to Victor Rothschild who passed it on to Dick White,[17] then head of MI6. There could then be no doubt that Philby had always been a double agent; even his staunchest supporters like Nicholas Elliott had to accept that for more than twenty years they had been completely bamboozled.[18]

The question then arose as to what should be done about Philby, and on this there was to be strong disagreement. At the top level Harold Macmillan, then prime minister, had a distaste for spies and wanted to have nothing to do with them. His expressed opinion was that they should not be prosecuted but left to rot and if possible turned into double agents. He was anxious to avoid another public scandal following the Blake affair and the earlier ones of Fuchs and Nunn May. He

17 Ex-schoolmaster of middle-class origins, at times head of both MI6 and MI5. Even-tempered and realistic but often in impossible situations.

18 In the words of the prophet Isaiah (35,5): 'Then the eyes of the blind shall be opened and the ears of the deaf unstopped.'

would have liked the whole business to be hushed up, but this could not be done.

Dick White, too, wanted to avoid a court case as it would show up the ineptitude and gullibility of MI6; but he wanted Philby to be punished after a thorough debriefing in which he could be compelled to reveal all his secrets. This too in part was the view of Nicholas Elliott, but he was ambivalent, brooding over other ways of dealing with the situation. It was eventually agreed that Elliott should interview Philby in Beirut and he should be offered immunity from prosecution in return for a full confession.

The ensuing confrontation was to be held in a small, heavily bugged sitting room of a secretary with the opponents fraught and seething but maintaining a lethal courtesy. Philby was still to be treated as an officer and a gentleman, but beneath the surface lay bitterness and steely resolve, Elliott making it clear that the game was up for Philby and MI6 had the whip hand, while Philby was giving away as little as possible and wondering whether to abscond to Russia or to continue the battle he had fought for so long and so keenly at home. He could not but realise that Elliott had him in his power and if he was to avoid arrest and life imprisonment he would have to do something he had never done before, make a partial confession revealing as little as possible; but little as this might be it was enough for Elliott to have him at his mercy.

The events of the following days brought confusion. Elliott departed, leaving the investigation of Philby to the man on the spot, Peter Lunn, who let it be known that he was going skiing. What were they up to? Were they laying a trap? Philby was left unguarded and free to take refuge in Russia if he desired. Was this what Elliott, backed perhaps by Dick White, had in mind? It seemed almost as if they were pushing him to Russia as the best means of disposing of him. It was a decision of which, for better or for worse, Philby was to avail himself. On 23 January 1963 with no interference from anyone he boarded a Russian cargo ship bound for Odessa disguised as a drunken Latvian seaman. It had been absurdly easy. Was this as it seemed rank incompetence on the part of MI6? Or was there more to it than met the eye? Philby left behind him a distraught and nonplussed wife and many in England and America with sharply conflicting opinions, some genuine, some simulated. In England there was indignation from some that Philby had been allowed to slip through the fingers of MI6. Dick White said that he was shocked; but seemed to be taking the matter calmly. Was he being disingenuous and complicit in Philby's escape? In America J. Edgar Hoover of the FBI was as angry as ever about what he regarded as British weakness and incompetence. James Angleton, head of the CIA, said he was dumbfounded and became demented. He could not believe that the man he had for so long trusted and befriended was a Soviet agent. He tried to make out that he had always had his suspicions, but this was unconvincing and easily disproved.

There was also some bewilderment in Russia. It had all been so easy. Was it a scheme engineered by MI6 to plant a treble agent full of disinformation? For a time Philby was kept under supervision, restricted in his movements and permanently under guard. It did not take him long to realise that he had little love for Moscow and was longing to be back in England among his favourite occupations – cricket scores and pub crawling. The KGB soon became aware that he had been a genuine Soviet agent, the best they were ever likely to have had, and tried to make life agreeable for him, allowing his third wife to join him and when she left, finding a fourth, Rufina Ivanova, twenty years younger of Polish stock. He was also to be commemorated by a place name in Moscow and portrayed on a postage stamp. But he was never to be happy. Somehow he had to come to terms with the reality that he had betrayed friends, family and all the things he loved most for a discredited creed.

He was to defend himself in a declaration that he had always operated on two levels, personal and political, and when the two came in conflict he had to put political first. He could also comfort himself with the thought that basic communism as laid down in the manifesto of 1848 – social equality, cooperation rather than competition, 'from each according to his ability, to each according to his needs' – still held good, although abused by power-hungry maniacs seeking a moral cover for their crimes. He died in 1988 at the age of seventy-six.

The uncovering of Philby was followed by the downfall of Anthony Blunt. He was the most erudite of the Cambridge Five, a distinguished art historian and academician, with a brilliant mind but indeterminate sex. During the Second World War he was co-opted into MI5 with access to vitally important secret information which he passed on to his Soviet handler. After the war he had a successful career becoming director of the Courtauld Institute, professor of history of art at London University, surveyor of the Queen's pictures and Sir Anthony Blunt KCVO. He would have liked to relinquish espionage but was to find that it was not easy to escape the KGB. In the early 1960s his treachery was suspected but it was not until 1964 that he was compelled to make a full confession on condition that he was granted immunity from prosecution. In 1979 he was denounced publicly by the then prime minister, Margaret Thatcher, stripped of his knighthood and dismissed from royal offices. In old age he was to admit to political naivety and that his involvement in communism was the greatest mistake of his life.

John Cairncross, the least publicised of the Cambridge Five, was always to keep a low profile. During the war he was taken on by MI5 and employed at Bletchley Park where he worked unobtrusively, sending to Moscow all he could, which was considerable. His role was gradually uncovered, mainly in the 1960s, when he made a series of partial confessions. He was never prosecuted, and was to be left to a quiet and inconspicuous retirement.

As has been seen the American agencies were highly critical of British intelligence, but they too were not free from spies and double agents. The Venona decrypts revealed that about 200 foreigners had been enlisted during the war, including some in the Treasury, the State Department and the nuclear Manhattan Project. In 1951 Julius and Ethel Rosenberg were found guilty of treasonable correspondence with a foreign power and sentenced to death by electrocution, and in the same year Alger Hiss, a former State Department official, was convicted of perjury for denying on oath that he had once been a communist and was sentenced to five years' imprisonment. Later others were to follow.

There were too Russian defectors from the KGB who looked longingly on freedom in the West as well as a much higher standard of living, but they were kept on a tight rein and knew only too well the fate that awaited them if they were caught.

CHAPTER SIX

FAR EAST

China past history – civil war – victory of communism – Chinese People's Republic – Mao Tse-Tung – Chiang Kai-shek to Formosa (Taiwan) – attitude of Stalin – Indian independence – separation of Pakistan – Commonwealth – independence of Dutch East Indies – war in Malaysia – settlement – Korean war – action of UN Security Council – dismissal of General Macarthur – Chinese intervention – deadlock – heavy toll of human life – consequences – Communist China excluded from UNO.

In 1948/49 a third world war was narrowly averted in Europe but one was to be more threatened in Asia. Communism is always to flourish most strongly where there is hunger, corruption and chaos, in which case it was bound to come to China. Once the proudest and most civilised country in the world, since the middle of the nineteenth century China had been reduced to weakness and humiliation. Foreign forces had invaded Chinese territory at will and imposed ignominious terms which gave them special rights and allowed them to annexe any part of the country which suited them. There was often no central government and much of China was dominated by local warlords and wealthy foreign merchants. In the 1920s one party had emerged as more powerful than others, the Kuomintang or Nationalist Party as it came to be called, led by Chiang Kai-shek, once an invoice clerk. But it could not control the whole country.

In 1934, after a historic Long March of 6,000 miles, a band of communist guerrillas reached part of China where nationalists could not get at them, initiating a civil war which was to last on and off for fourteen years. The leader of this group was Mao Tse-Tung, an ex-librarian and an aspiring poet. He was a leader of genius, destined to rule a quarter of the human race for a quarter of a century. In 1937 China was invaded by Japan, which by 1938 had occupied most of the eastern seaboard. For a time both nationalists and communists fought against the Japanese and the civil war went into abeyance, but with the sudden surrender of Japan in 1945 following the atom bombs on Hiroshima and Nagasaki, it was to break out again and to last for three years. At first it seemed the communists had little chance of victory: they were outnumbered two to one, had no air or naval forces and no help from abroad. However, they were not to be subdued; their morale was high; they believed passionately in their cause and were winning the hearts and minds of the Chinese people. By contrast the fighting spirit of the nationalists was low and dejected – hungry, uninspired and under-paid (if at all) they resorted to looting local inhabitants who associated them with rich warlords and foreign intruders. Many were deserting to the communists, taking with them arms and equipment which had been provided for them by the United States. By 1948 the communists were everywhere in the ascendant and final victory came at the end of 1949 when

Chiang resigned the presidency and withdrew with the forces still loyal to him to the island of Formosa (later Taiwan) to carry on some sort of resistance from there. At the same time Mao in Peking proclaimed the establishment of the Chinese People's Republic and set about creating a new China and a world power at the cost of several million lives. In this he had no aid from Russia. Stalin regarded him with suspicion, a possible rival whom he could not tolerate. It seemed he preferred a weak, divided China under the nationalists rather than a strong communist state under Mao.

It was likely that communism, having overwhelmed China, would spread to other countries in Asia. Certainly, pre-war European colonialism was coming to an end, impelled by both Russia and America. Britain was to lead the way. Weakened by six years of war and an economy verging on bankruptcy and the rapid growth of Indian nationalism, the post-war Labour government was to grant independence to India in 1947. There were those who thought that this was overdue, but when it happened it was to cause widespread upheavals; owing to religious differences millions were to lose their lives or become homeless refugees. Independence also brought about a division of the subcontinent into two nations – India, primarily Hindu; and Pakistan, Muslim. Conditions were such that they might seem to be ripe for communist takeovers, but these did not come; democratic governments were to be set up, republics declared and they were to remain in the newly formed Commonwealth.[19] This marked the final development of what had been the British Empire. The British monarch was acknowledged as head of it but all member countries were equal and independent. All they had in common was that they had once been British

19 This had been formed in 1949 consisting of states regardless of race, some rich, some struggling. Between 1945 and 1968 the number of them increased from five to twenty-eight.

colonies. A few years later India was to become the world's largest democracy and had gained a prominent position on the world stage as a dominant force in the Non-Aligned Countries which sought to arbitrate in the Cold War.

Subsequently other British colonies in Asia were to follow in the same direction. After prolonged belligerence, communist guerrillas in Malaysia were overcome and a democratic regime instituted. In 1965 Singapore, an island south of the Malayan peninsula and a British colony since 1819, became the independent State of Singapore within the Commonwealth and in 1997 sovereignty of the British crown colony of Hong Kong was transferred to the Republic of China – these two, arguably, the most prosperous and invigorated states in Asia.

The course of other European powers in the dissolution of their Asian empires was to be less peaceful. In the Dutch East Indies, comprising some 2,000 islands, the leader of the Nationalist movement, Achmet Sukarno, who had collaborated with the Japanese during the war, was to proclaim the Independent Republic of Indonesia in 1945. This the Dutch refused to recognise and three years of war ensued at the end of which, partly owing to pressure from the United States and the United Nations, the Dutch had to give way. In French Indo-China which comprised Cambodia, Laos and Vietnam, there was a longer and more bitter struggle.

There were to be communist insurrections in other parts of Asia, but these were soon subdued apart from that in Malaya where there was to be a prolonged struggle before British and Malayan forces finally prevailed. At first the communists gained the upper hand: strikes were called, trains derailed and officials murdered; also attacks were made on rubber plantations on which the wealth of the country depended, trees being slashed and workers killed or terrorised. A British response to these tactics was delayed and it was not until 1950 that effective countermeasures were taken. By then rubber estates, tin mines and all outlying communities were turned into armed camps while communist forces were isolated and cut off from food supplies and foreign aid but it was realised that the main battle would be for 'the hearts and minds' of the people (of mixed races – British, Indians, Malays and Chinese) and this was greatly enhanced when an undertaking came from the British government that Malaya would now proceed towards self-government. This had a widespread effect on public opinion and did much to take the wind out of the communists' sails. From then on all anti-communist forces could feel that they were fighting for a free and independent Malaysia, not just the continuation of British rule. By 1954 the communists had been almost overcome but, although hungry, demoralised and heavily outnumbered, they continued to fight on, and the war did not finally end until 1960.

In 1950 open warfare broke out in Asia when the Democratic Republic of North Korea invaded the South Korean Republic. It might have seemed improbable that the Korean peninsula would be the part of the world which nearly precipitated a third world war. Known as 'the Land of the Morning Calm', it had been part of the Japanese Empire since 1910. At the end of the Second World War it was occupied by both American and Russian forces, and for the sake of convenience was divided at random into two parts along the 38th line of latitude, the north under the Russians and the south under the Americans. This division was not meant to be permanent and it was expected that in time the country would be reunited under a government of its own choice. This, however, was prevented by the Russians who, despite a United Nations resolution, refused to allow free elections in the north which would almost certainly have been anti-communist. And so the two parts remained separate.

Chinese troops pouring into North Korea to
oppose forces of United Nations, 1951.

In the last years of the war, on the instigation of President Roosevelt, a new international organisation was set up to replace the old League of Nations and which would be responsible for keeping the peace of the world. The United Nations Organisation (UNO as it was called) came into being in 1945 when fifty nations signed its charter in San Francisco. It was to have a General Assembly in which all countries had equal voting rights, but the task of keeping the peace fell mainly on the Security Council in which there were five permanent members – the United States, Russia, Britain, France and China (of Chiang Kai-shek rather than Mao Tse-Tung). On Russian insistence no decision could be taken unless all of these agreed, which meant in effect that each of the permanent members had the right to block, or 'veto', a decision. This was resented by smaller countries, some of which lost faith in it and were disposed to take independent action.

The invasion of North Korea was the first time the Security Council was called on to take a critical decision. It was a challenge it could not afford to ignore. In similar circumstances in 1935 the League of Nations had failed to support Abyssinia when that country was invaded by Italy. If in 1950 the Security Council could only resort to heated talk and uneasy compromises its reputation would be fatally impaired.

As it happened the United States government took prompt and effective action. President Truman summoned a meeting of the Security Council which passed a resolution calling for a ceasefire and the withdrawal of the North Koreans. These resolutions would certainly have been vetoed by the Russians if they had been present, but at the time they were boycotting the United Nations because of its refusal to admit communist China. The Security Council also passed a resolution promising all necessary assistance to the South

Koreans. It was considered by most countries that the action of the North Koreans was open aggression, and altogether fifty countries pledged support, although only fourteen of these eventually were to send forces to fight in Korea. Of these the great majority were American. The British force, sent by the Labour government, was the second largest.

The Korean War proved to be an up and down affair. At first the armies of the north carried all before them and overran the whole country apart from a defensive peninsula round the port of Pusan in the extreme south. But then the tide turned and the UN Supreme Commander, General MacArthur,[20] carried out a bold operation, landing forces nearly 200 miles behind the enemy lines, thus threatening to cut them off. This resulted in the defeat of the North Korean army which by the end of September 1950 had been driven back across the 38th parallel.

At this point a crucial decision had to be taken. Should the United Nations consider their task to be completed? Or were they to invade North Korea and bring about the reunion of the two parts of the country? To do so would involve risk of war with Russia or China or both. President Truman was cautious, as were other UN leaders, notably Clement Attlee, the British prime minister; but MacArthur urged it strongly and managed to get his way, and so on 1 October UN forces crossed into North Korea. At first all went well and MacArthur expected the war to be over by Christmas; but then came Chinese intervention. Mao Tse-Tung decided that this should be on a large scale; it would be the best way of weakening the United States and allied armies. He had at his command a massive reserve of 'cannon fodder' which did not need to be spared, and so-called 'volunteers' were

20 General Douglas MacArthur was a great hero in the United States because of the heroic defence by his army against the Japanese forces invading the Philippines in 1941–42. Since the end of the war he had been the supreme power in Japan.

poured into North Korea in increasing numbers irrespective of losses. This changed the nature of the war completely. The UN force found itself in an entirely different situation, confronted with a new, powerful army being supplied from bases in Manchuria which could not be bombed. In the following months the UN forces were pushed back into South Korea; but then the position stabilised.

The Americans and their allies with superior fire power were able again to force the Chinese back across the 38th parallel on 3 April 1951. It was then that there was a serious disagreement between President Truman and General MacArthur: the latter wanted to extend the war to China, bring in the forces of Chiang Kai-shek from Taiwan and, if necessary, to use atomic weapons. Truman, strongly supported by the British and others, was opposed to this, maintaining that open war should be avoided, that it was necessary only to 'contain' communist aggression, and the reuniting of the two parts of Korea should be abandoned. In the end this difference became so acute that in April 1951 Truman felt he had to dismiss MacArthur, an act requiring great courage because of MacArthur's legendary reputation. By July 1951 it was evident that a deadlock had been reached and the first armistice talks took place, but no agreement could be obtained, and the war was to drag on for another two years until July 1953, by which time Stalin had died and been replaced by more moderate leadership, while Truman had been replaced as president by General Eisenhower who let it be known that if a treaty was not signed, he might be prepared to use nuclear weapons. And so in July 1953 a peace treaty was finally agreed by which Korea remained divided. A negative result.

The Korean War took a heavy toll of human life: 142,000 Americans, 300,000 South Koreans and perhaps as many as two million Chinese and North Koreans – a heavy price for what had been gained: the authority of the United Nations had been upheld, aggression frustrated and South Korea saved from communism. On the other hand relations between the United States and communist China had been critically aborted. But for the Korean War America might not have withheld recognition of communist China and given support to Chiang Kai-shek or Taiwan. For the time being the most populous country in the world was to be excluded on American insistence from the community of nations.

CHAPTER SEVEN

MIDDLE EAST

Britain dominant at end of war – mandates for Iraq, Transjordan and Palestine from UNO – too much to bear – Arab-Israeli Conflict – hostility in America – British rule in Egypt – Suez Canal – rise of Gamal Nasser – British withdrawal – nationalisation of Suez Canal – Anglo-French-Israeli invasion meets opposition of US and others – forced withdrawal – blow to Western unity – dependence on US emphasised – power of oil-producing countries (OPEC) – threat to Israel – Six-Day War – Yom Kippur War – Israel victorious – Camp David agreement – Egypt under Sadat comes to terms.

In the war against communism the Western Allies usually presented a united front. In Europe they had joined together in NATO, and in the Far East they had rallied to the lead of the United States in the war in Korea. But differences did arise and nowhere more so than in the Middle East. There at the end of the Second World War, Britain was still the dominant power. Its colonies amounted to no more than Cyprus and Aden, but it had been granted mandates by the United Nations for the administration of Iraq, Transjordan and Palestine; it was also in a commanding position in Egypt. Weakened by six years of war, however, and with little economic clout, these responsibilities had become beyond Britain's capabilities. Its power in world affairs was declining and the United States was not always supportive. In 1951 when the United Kingdom became embroiled in a dispute with the government of Iran about the nationalisation of the Anglo-Iranian Oil Company there was little help from America, rather the reverse.

Britain's mandate over Palestine proved an impossible task: in effect it was to act as arbiter and peacemaker between two bitterly opposed forces – those of Jewish and Arab nationalism. Britain's involvement in Palestine began in 1917 in the middle of the First World War when the country was in a desperate plight and in need of international alliances and the foreign secretary, Arthur Balfour, declared British support for a small Jewish national home in Palestine provided that 'safeguards could be reached for the rights of non-Jewish communities in Palestine.' This Balfour Declaration, as it came to be called, was later confirmed by all Allied governments. If it had remained as originally defined it might have been the basis for a viable settlement but it was to assume disproportionate significance. At the end of the Second World War there were about a million displaced Jews in Europe who had escaped the Nazi holocaust and thought there was an opportunity for establishing a homeland in the territory of their, by then distant, forefathers. On the other hand there were Arabs who had been living in Palestine for over a thousand years and were determined not to be overrun by a nation of Europeanised Jews in their midst. Britain's attempts to bring together the two sides resulted in both becoming hostile – the Jews because Britain was limiting immigration from Europe, the Arabs because too many were being let in. Britain's relations with the United States were also to be strained because of a strong and vocal Jewish body of support particularly in New York; and in other quarters there was concern that European Jews might seek to emigrate to America rather than to Palestine.

In 1948 it became necessary for Britain to give up the mandate. This was followed at once by the proclamation of the State of Israel and war between Jews and Arabs, brought to an end temporarily and indecisively by the intervention of the United Nations.

After giving up the mandate, Britain was to maintain a voice in Middle Eastern affairs due in part to its standing in Egypt. Egypt had never been a British colony. It had once been a province of the Turkish Empire, governed by a Khedive appointed by the Sultan. But in 1883 Britain was drawn into occupying the country when it lapsed into bankruptcy and anarchy. This was intended to be a temporary measure until order was restored but, as it turned out, British rule in Egypt lasted for seventy years. This was due largely to Turkey taking the side of Germany in the First World War but more so because of the vital importance to Britain of the Suez Canal. Opened in 1869, this had more than halved the distance for shipping to India and the Far East as well as to Arabia. The construction of the canal had been mainly the work of the French who with the Egyptians had been the original owners; but an Egyptian Khedive, ever in financial straits, had been willing to sell his shares in the company which had been on offer and taken up promptly by the British Prime Minister Benjamin Disraeli. Later, Britain was to institute what was called a Protectorate in Egypt. After the First World War there was a surge in Egyptian nationalism and the cry of 'Egypt for the Egyptians' was heard increasingly. The British took heed of this but were unwilling to leave the country completely because of the need to protect the Suez Canal. In 1922 Egypt was declared an independent sovereign state, and in 1936 all British forces were evacuated apart from a garrison in the Canal Zone. This arrangement lasted until after the Second World War when Egyptian national feelings were inflamed by the establishment of the State of Israel and the failure of the subsequent war to eradicate it. In 1952 there was a coup activated by a group of military officers who expelled the westernised Egyptian King Farouk and instituted an Egyptian republic. In 1954 this became dominated by a forcefully ambitious young officer of thirty-four, Gamal Nasser.

Nasser was to be the main power in Egyptian (and Arab) politics for the next thirteen years. His main objectives were the extinction of the State of Israel, the evacuation of British forces from the Canal Zone and the general aggrandisement of Egypt. He was particularly interested in expanding Egyptian agriculture by the construction of a giant dam across the Nile at the city of Aswan, a highly expensive project needing large-scale foreign aid. For a time it seemed possible that this might be forthcoming from the United States, but it was withdrawn suddenly when Nasser became too closely involved with communist countries; whereupon he announced that the cost of the dam would be met by the nationalisation of the Suez Canal Company. This was a drastic step, and for the British Prime Minister Sir Anthony Eden, totally unacceptable. To him it was a breach of an international treaty and an illegal act. To allow Nasser to get away with it amounted to appeasement of a dictator. He became convinced that Nasser was out for what he could get by any means, that his aim was the leadership of the Arab world and the extinction of the State of Israel; and it was intolerable that one of the world's main waterways, of vital importance to Britain and all Western countries, should be under the control of a volatile Egyptian despot. 'Nasser must not be allowed,' he declared, 'to have his thumb on our windpipe.' For these reasons he decided that this was an occasion when force might have to be used.

For Eden this was out of character. As foreign secretary, a post he had held for ten years, he had a reputation for cool judgement and diplomatic ability. However, by 1956, following a major surgical operation, his health had declined, and he was apt to be nervy and unbalanced, too inclined to go his own way without reference to colleagues or advisors. In this condition he was to be drawn into an ill-judged stratagem with the Israelis and the French to bring Nasser down.[21] This, conducted in secrecy, provided that Israel, still formally at war with Egypt, would make a pre-emptive strike into the country, and Britain and France would intervene as peacemakers and impose terms which included regaining control of the Suez Canal. If Nasser rejected these terms he would be coerced by the bombing of Egyptian targets and the landing of forces in the Canal Zone. These operations were to take place in secret and might have been successful, but when news of them broke there was uproar. Many, including some in Britain and France, who had been kept in the dark, were deeply shocked and could hardly believe that it was happening. Most foreign countries, even European allies and members of the Commonwealth, disapproved and the United States, for once in agreement with Soviet Russia, took the lead and was not only critical but actively hostile, bringing to bear its overwhelming economic forces on Britain and France to end hostilities. At the same time Khrushchev took the opportunity to talk menacingly of the use of rocket weapons. Thus faced with hostile world opinion, loud opposition at

21 The French were strongly averse to Nasser because of his aid to subversive forces in their colony of Algeria.

home and the imminent collapse of the pound, with the value of sterling declining dramatically, Britain and France had to give way and make a humiliating withdrawal.

This ruthless treatment by President Eisenhower of two of America's main allies in the Cold War was, as he later admitted, a grave error. He had overreacted. He could not but have been in agreement with the purpose of the Anglo-French-Israeli operation – to safeguard the State of Israel and to protect the Suez Canal, and though he might have objected to their plan of action he needed to have done no more than disavow it, holding aloof and speaking bluntly in private, but not to have gone to extremes and coerced them into defeat by the threat of bankruptcy. His policy in the Middle East was ambivalent: on the one hand pro-Israel and anti-Nasser, on the other favouring oil-rich Arab states and convincing them of the benefits of American democracy rather than communist despotism.

The Suez Affair was a major blow to the capitalist cause, nearly bringing about the breakdown of the Western Alliance. As a result Nasser was not deposed and became for a time a hero in the Arab world; he also retained possession of the Suez Canal. Russian influence in the area was to increase and there was a rift among Western powers at a time when unity was especially needed to confront the Russians over their treatment of Poland and Hungary. For Britain and France and other members of NATO there was the reality which had to be faced that in the modern world all depended on the United States. Independent action without them could not be undertaken.

The Middle East was to become increasingly a bone of contention between communism and capitalism. Nowhere was more vital because it was the world's greatest source of oil on which all countries were becoming more and more dependent while the countries producing it were becoming ever more aware of their power. In 1961 the Organisation of Petroleum Exporting Countries (OPEC) was formed to assist their members in its dealings with the multinationals (such as Shell, Esso and British Petroleum). Here OPEC was to gain the whip hand and it was to use its power to coerce Western governments to give up their support of Israel. They were determined 'to drive Israel into the sea' and to restore Palestine to what it had been before mass Jewish immigration. That would have been a calamitous blow to America which had been instrumental in setting up the State of Israel and where there was strong support for it. President Nasser of Egypt was to take the lead in this.

In 1967 he amassed an invasion army on the Israeli border at the same time as the Syrians and Jordanians prepared to invade Israel from their countries. These states had been armed with modern weapons by the Russians and it seemed that Israel must be overwhelmed; but it had had military aid from the United States, it had superior expertise and fought with passionate intensity. It was to strike first with devastating effect. The Egyptian Air Force was destroyed on the ground and its army driven out of the Sinai Peninsula. At the same time the Syrians were evicted from the Golan Heights and the Jordanians from the West Bank of the Jordan and their part of Jerusalem. The Six-Day War, as it came to be called, resulted in extensive territorial gains for Israel, as well as 600,000 more Arabs coming under their jurisdiction.

Six years later in 1973 on the Jewish holy day of Yom Kippur (Day of Atonement) Egyptian and Syrian armies with support from Jordan, Iraq and Saudi Arabia again launched attacks on Israel. Because it was a holy day the Israeli forces were caught off guard and for a time the situation for them was critical; but aid from America was flown in and the Israeli forces rallied and counter-attacked. As a result the invading Egyptian army was cut in two and the Israelis crossed the

Suez Canal into Egypt. The Syrians too were halted, and soon afterwards the United Nations called for a ceasefire and a peacekeeping force was brought into the area to keep the opposing armies apart.

There were far-reaching consequences from the 'Yom Kippur War'. President Sadat of Egypt, who had become president in 1971 on the death of Nasser, came to realise that agreement had to be reached with Israel. Egypt was not a rich country and could not afford a state of permanent war. Also Egypt had no direct interest in annihilating Israel; there were no overriding reasons why the two countries should not live at peace. So in 1977 Sadat visited Jerusalem and proposed peace talks; and in the following year he and the Israeli Prime Minister Menachem Begin met in America under the auspices of President Carter at his residence in Camp David and came to an agreement which was signed in 1979. For this Sadat was to be attacked bitterly by other Arab leaders,[22] as was Begin by Jewish extremists. Not all outstanding matters were settled at Camp David, but at least Israel's right to exist was acknowledged, and it marked the withdrawal of Egypt from the Arab-Israeli conflict. In this it was a notable capitalist success.

22 He was assassinated in 1981.

CHAPTER EIGHT

EUROPE POST-STALIN

Stalin, power of — rise of Khrushchev — denunciation of Stalin — brinkmanship – Bulganin and Khrushchev to England – Buster Crabb – Wladyslaw in Poland – Imre Nagy in Hungary – revolt crushed – racial discrimination in US – drawbacks of superpower (Korea, Vietnam) – Castro in Cuba – French in Algeria – General de Gaulle rejection of British claim to join Common Market – decline of de Gaulle – Britain into Common Market (1972).

In 1953 the course of the Cold War was to change with the death of Stalin, the mighty dictator who had presided over the transformation of a primarily agrarian Russia into a modern industrial giant; and then been the main force in the defeat of fascism and the subjection of Eastern Europe to the dominance of communism. He had also been responsible for the deaths of many millions. No Russian had ever wielded such power, far greater than that of the tsars; his authority stretched from the Baltic to the Pacific. His rule was absolute, extending over all aspects of ordinary life; academics and writers were compelled to keep rigidly to his dictates; history was rewritten to fit in with his image; even art and music were dominated by his tastes, all western influences being banned.

In the same year, Dwight Eisenhower, after long and meritorious service to America and the world as supreme allied commander in the invasion of Europe in the Second World War and later of the forces of NATO, became president of the United States. As such, for eight years he had at his command an arsenal of weaponry which could obliterate civilisation.[23] It was an awesome responsibility: in what circumstances should these nuclear weapons be used? What if Stalin or his successors with their vastly larger conventional armies were to invade Western Europe? His finger was on the trigger. He knew the consequences. What Churchill called the equality of annihilation. Destruction of the enemy but likely suicide for oneself.

Stalin's death was followed by a struggle among his subordinates from which by 1955 Nikita Khrushchev emerged as first secretary of the Communist Party and main power in the land. A man of humble origins, son of a miner and one himself for a time, he had been to the fore during the Revolution and been responsible for crushing resistance in the Ukraine where he had become known as 'the butcher'. He was of a different calibre from Stalin – voluble, indiscreet, impulsive, at times rational and temperate, at others blustering and pugnacious. This was the man on whom the future of humanity was to some extent to depend.

In 1956 in the Twentieth Congress of the Communist Party he made a long and forthright denunciation of Stalin

23 In 1952, the US exploded the first hydrogen bomb, said to have 100 times the explosive force of those dropped on Nagasaki and Hiroshima.

and Stalinism, accusing him of flagrant abuse of power, brutality and wilfulness. He also blamed him for perversion of true communism by promoting the cult of the individual and for Russia's unpreparedness for war at the time of the German invasion in 1941. As can be imagined the speech caused a sensation; the sudden villainising of the man whom Russians had been brought up to regard as 'the wise father of all peoples' brought dismay and confusion in the ranks of communism: some welcoming it, some deeply shocked. Khrushchev was able to ease some of the harsher elements of Stalinism – curtailing the activities of the secret police, releasing political prisoners, even talking at times of 'differing ways to socialism' and peaceful coexistence with democracy. However, he was to realise that in sanctioning liberal measures he was releasing forces he might not be able to control. Once having been given a taste of freedom people were going to want more and, if this was given, the dictatorship of the Communist Party would be endangered. He therefore felt it necessary to hold back and to make it clear that there were limits to the freedom that could be expected from him and that he was a man of iron as well as a moderate reformer. His more pragmatic prosecution of the Cold War and liberal measures in Russia had been strongly opposed by the Russian old guard who stuck to despotism and dogma and he had to show that his policies bore fruit. In doing so he became involved in perilous adventures abroad which came to be known as 'brinkmanship'. In pursuit of this he was to be loud-mouthed and aggressive and making sure that the world was aware of Soviet nuclear power. At the same time he backed away from a third world war as he knew its consequences and the significance of 'mutual destruction'.

1956 was to be a turbulent year in the Cold War, abounding in crises and clashes. Khrushchev's denunciation of Stalin in January was followed by an uprising in Poland in June, and in October a major revolt in Hungary. At the same time there was the disastrous Suez affair.

In April Khrushchev and his prime minister Nikolai Bulganin (described as his 'mouthpiece') went on an unfortunate visit to England at the invitation of Sir Anthony Eden who had succeeded Churchill as Britain's prime minister in the previous year. It was hoped that it would engender goodwill but there was to be little of this. It stirred up strong opposition from anti-communist forces which held a mass meeting of protest from which was issued a terse statement:

Closer relations with Russia could no longer exist so long as the Soviet remained communist, retaining prisoners of war, maintaining slave labour camps and continuing to hold in thrall the nations of Eastern Europe.

The main instigator of this movement was Malcolm Muggeridge whose sharp acerbic wit was to deride the idea that the Russian leaders might reform their ideas as a result of seeing democratic ways of life.[24] The Russians were to have a somewhat uneasy visit to Oxford University during which the warden of New College was to show them with pride a sculpture of *Lazarus* by Jacob Epstein in the college chapel of which Khrushchev said that it was 'decadent bourgeois art' and gave him nightmares.[25] He was also unappreciative of undergraduate humour when a group waiting for him to pass broke into a song lamenting the death of Old Black Joe. As it was only a few months since he had denounced Josef Stalin he thought this an impertinence and showed it.

There was a calamity during their visit when British intelligence (MI6) sought to investigate the underwater

24 He was to ridicule such a notion: 'This was like bringing two professional ladies from *Moulin Rouge* to attend Roedean School in the hope that they will marry archdeacons and settle down to a life of quiet respectability.'

25 To which Epstein was to retort that Khrushchev should 'stick to murder and leave art to artists.'

structure of the modern Russian warship which had brought Khrushchev and Bulganin to England. Eden had given orders that during their visit there should be no espionage; but this was disobeyed by MI6 which engaged a special frogman, Lionel Crabb (known as 'Buster'), to find out what he could. The operation was to go disastrously wrong. It seems the Russians got wind of what was going on and disposed of Crabb who disappeared and was not heard of again until his partially decomposed corpse was discovered by fishermen nearby a few months later.

The riots which broke out in Poland in 1956 arose from the hope of more independence: Wladyslaw Gomulka, a communist leader who had been purged by Stalin in 1948 and imprisoned ever since, was elected first secretary of the Communist Party, at which Russian leaders took fright and ordered Russian tanks to move in. Gomulka was able to persuade Khrushchev that he had no intention of taking Poland out of the Warsaw Pact, and the Russian forces withdrew without bloodshed. He was to remain in office for fourteen years during which he pursued a finely balanced policy of keeping Soviet authorities at bay and decommunising Poland, ending agricultural collectivisation, restricting the activities of the secret police and toning down Soviet-inspired Five-Year Plans benefiting Russia more than Poland; but he had not been able to go as far as he would have liked, lost popular support and in 1970 was compelled to resign.

1956 also saw a major insurrection in Hungary. No member of the Warsaw Pact had been more resentful of Russian domination. Hungary by then was what remained of the Dual Monarchy of Austria-Hungary, once the most powerful nation in Europe, but in the First World War it had fought on the side of Germany and was treated vindictively at the end of it. In the Treaty of Trianon the Dual Monarchy was abolished, the country deprived of two-thirds of its territory and its population reduced from about twenty million to eight.

In a general election in 1945 a majority was gained by the non-communist Smallholders Party, but this was soon to be ousted by the United Workers' Party led by Matyas Rákosi, a committed Moscow-trained communist. He was to head a Stalinist administration from 1945 to 1956. By then it had become widely unpopular; Hungarian nationalism was surfacing, there was smouldering resentment at the terms of the Trianon Treaty, and bitter feelings about occupation of the country by alien forces. There was a growing determination for the country to break away from the Warsaw Pact and join the ranks of Non-Aligned Nations. On 23 October 1956 there was an outburst of angry protest in Budapest with the tumbling and destruction of an enormous statue of Stalin. This was followed by a new administration led by moderate communists Imre Nagy and Janos Kadar which relaxed communist measures and let in more private enterprise; but on 31 October Nagy went too far and too fast when he announced Hungary's withdrawal from the Warsaw Pact. This caused a break with Kadar and a decision by Khrushchev that Hungary could not be allowed to go its own way. And so Russian tanks were sent into Budapest where hard and bitter fighting took place. The Russians were ruthless and in ten days all resistance had been overcome. As a result of the rebellion some 25,000 Hungarians were killed, 30,000 wounded and about 140,000 became refugees.

Before the fighting ended the Hungarians sent an appeal for help to the United Nations and all free people everywhere, but there was no effective response. The only way in which the West could have intervened to save Hungary was by nuclear war and this was too great a price to pay. The lesson to be learned from the Hungarian uprising was that the

Russians under Khrushchev were not prepared to let any of the satellite countries out of their control, they were ready to invade and use force, and there was little the Western Allies could do about it. The only help the people of Eastern Europe could expect from the West was moral support. For the time being there could be little change in the Hungarian situation. Although this represented a victory for communists it was short term; it did not last. In the long term it was to tell against them. The tyranny and brutality of Marxist-Leninism had been exposed to freedom-loving people everywhere.

One of Eisenhower's main aims as president was to win the support of Third World countries and persuade them that American democracy was superior to the despotic regimes of communism. In this he could be ruthless as when for a time he prevented US citizens with left-wing views from leaving the country in case they spread adverse views abroad.[26] It was also why he took such drastic action in the Suez affair of 1956. To have done otherwise, he said, would have lost the goodwill in all Arabia (of increasing importance because of its virtually unlimited source of oil). In taking such a stance on behalf of Third World countries rather than the colonial powers like Britain and France Eisenhower was open to the charge of duplicity; the records of United States administrations since the war in home affairs had hardly been exemplary.

In the Declaration of Independence of 1776 on which the American constitution was founded it was laid down that 'all men are equal and entitled to life, liberty and the pursuit of happiness.' But there were millions of African Americans being treated as second-class citizens, restricted as to where they lived, how they travelled and limited to lesser jobs. To

26 The great singer and entertainer Paul Robeson was confined in the United States without a passport for eight years.

win their support during the Second World War they had been led to believe that with the coming of peace there would be a new deal for them, but there were few signs of this. The general trend was to revert to 'rugged individualism' which meant in effect pushing one's own interests at the expense of all others. The situation of African Americans had not improved greatly: segregation was rife and brutal crimes were being perpetrated against them as the Ku Klux Klan ran riot with lynchings and torchlight processions. The movement for equal rights was progressing slowly under the inspiration of Martin Luther King, Baptist minister and visionary leader, but was held back by old prejudices and fears.

During his presidency Eisenhower was to find that there were serious drawbacks to being a superpower – so many dependents in different parts of the world were looking for protection and financial aid. After the victory of the communists in mainland China Chiang Kai-shek in Taiwan insisted on an American guarantee with nuclear weapons if necessary, not only in Taiwan but also in the offshore islands of Quemoy and Matso, described by Secretary of State Foster Dulles as 'a bunch of rocks', hardly worth the risk of a nuclear war. Also to stress dependence on the United States was President Syngman Rhee of South Korea in coming to terms with the aggressive communists of the north; and President Ngo Dinh Diem of South Vietnam in confronting another communist regime in the north – these were examples of what came to be known as 'the tail wagging the dog'. Nearer home there was a grave danger in the Caribbean island of Cuba, some ninety miles off the American coast. There in 1956 Fidel Castro, a former law student and active revolutionary recently released from gaol for subversive activities, landed on the island with eighty-two followers and embarked on guerrilla warfare to bring down the corrupt and despotic regime of Fulgencia Batista. It seemed a desperate venture but in the course of the next two years he won the support of thousands of Cubans and in 1959 entered Havana, the capital, and was then to be the country's dictator for the next fifty years, a constant thorn in the flesh of United States administrations. This problem Eisenhower was to bequeath to John F. Kennedy when he became president in 1961.

During Eisenhower's presidency the countries of Western Europe were reinforced in 1956 by the admission of West Germany (then the Federal Republic of Germany) into NATO. In 1957 they were further bound together by the Treaty of Rome which was to lead to the establishment of the Common Market although from this Britain was at first to stand apart. In the following years the Common Market was to thrive with trade between member countries increasing, their industries expanding, and the standard of living of their peoples becoming conspicuously higher. This rapid development of one of the world's largest trading groups so close at hand could not be ignored by the British; many were having a change of heart, and in 1961 the Conservative government of Harold Macmillan applied for membership. This was a bold act as there was strong opposition to it in some quarters and it might have led to the break-up of the Conservative Party, but in the event Britain's application was turned down. Previously it would have been welcome but that was before the re-emergence on the scene of General de Gaulle.

General de Gaulle was a man of destiny, of which no one was more aware than himself. At the fall of France in 1940, although only a junior general, he proclaimed himself head of the Free French who would continue the war against Germany, irrespective of the government of Marshal Pétain in Vichy. As such he was accepted by Churchill, although he was to be an awkward collaborator, making frequent difficulties, standing on his dignity and overstepping the mark. President Roosevelt developed a strong aversion to him and attempts were made to replace him, but as was to be seen in later life, he was a great survivor. At the liberation of France in 1945 he was given a hero's welcome and elected president of the newly established Fourth Republic, but because he was not granted enough power he resigned after only ten weeks and went into retirement. He expected to be recalled soon as France's saviour, but for this he had to wait eleven years.

In 1958 France was on the verge of civil war on account of the chaotic condition in Algeria, a French colony in which there was a large French European population.[27] As in all European colonies after the Second World War, there was a widespread growth of nationalism and most colonies had gained their independence, but in France there was a strong feeling that if the country was to regain its position as a world power it had to have colonies and these had to be retained at all costs. The consequence of this was long-running guerrilla warfare between the French army and the Algerian *Front de la Liberation Nationale (FLN)*. In 1958 when a new French government seemed to be about to come to terms with the rebels, the leaders of the European population there, backed by the army, took matters into their own hands, defying the French government, and even threatening the invasion of France.

In this desperate situation de Gaulle felt that the time had come to intervene. He proceeded to act in a way that was high-handed, adroit and devious. He was able thus to introduce a new republic, the fifth, in which the president had more power and parliament less. Thus strengthened, he dealt with the Algerian crisis. Previously he had given a pledge

---

27 Amounting to about one million as opposed to about eight million Algerians of Arab descent.

that Algeria would always be French, but then he did an about turn and announced that the country had to be independent. This caused fury in some quarters and there were a number of attempts on his life but, as always, he proved indestructible. The majority of French people were convinced that he was the only person who could save France from disruption and rallied to his support in a referendum with an overwhelming majority.

He was then to turn his attention to the subject nearest to his heart – rebuilding the power and glory of France in the world. He had not at first been favourably disposed towards the Common Market and made it clear that in matters concerning France he was not to be overruled by a majority of other countries, but he also realised that it could serve his main purpose. He saw that France on its own carried little weight in world affairs, but at the head of the Common Market it was a force with which to be reckoned. He was therefore only interested in the Common Market provided it was dominated by France, and for this reason he was firmly opposed to the admission of Britain. That would have meant shared leadership with French leadership correspondingly diminished. Macmillan's application he tried to prevent first by delaying tactics, making endless difficulties and seeing to it that negotiations went on as long as possible in the hope that opposition in Britain to the Common Market might increase and support for it lapse. But this did not happen. Britain's chief negotiator, Edward Heath (subsequently prime minister 1970–74), was able and persistent as well as an ardent European and in the end all outstanding matters were settled. It was then that de Gaulle revealed himself in his true colours and declared that he was opposed to British membership in principle on the grounds that Britain was not 'European minded', and her ties with the United States and the Commonwealth were too great, so he imposed a veto which he was entitled to do. This came as a shock to Macmillan who thought with some reason that he had been deceived. If de Gaulle objected in principle he should have said so at the beginning of negotiations, not at the end.

Britain's second application to join the Common Market came six years later during the Labour administration of Harold Wilson who tried to persuade de Gaulle to change his mind; but in vain. This time he did not allow negotiations to begin; he imposed a veto at once. By then, however, his time was running out. For ten years he had been the dominant force in Western Europe. Besides blocking Britain's entry into the Common Market, he had been adversarial towards America, had distanced France from NATO by withdrawing some French forces, made bilateral agreements with West Germany and Russia and went his own way imperiously. His rule ended following widespread and prolonged demonstrations by students and workers in Paris in May 1968. He won a subsequent general election but in 1969 his proposed reforms were rejected in a referendum and he resigned. He died the following year.

De Gaulle was succeeded by Georges Pompidou who was less intransigent. In 1970 a Conservative government came into office in Britain under Edward Heath and detailed talks began again. A year later agreement was reached and on 22 January 1972 Britain (with Ireland and Denmark) signed a treaty of accession to the European Community. In 1975 when Harold Wilson became prime minister again, a referendum was held which showed a two-thirds majority in favour of British membership.

CHAPTER NINE

THE KHRUSHCHEV ERA

US spy plane – Khrushchev leaves summit – J.F. Kennedy as President – Berlin crisis – Khrushchev ultimatum – flow; of refugees from East – Berlin Wall – Castro in Cuba – Bay of Pigs – Russian missile bases – Cuba into quarantine – threat of Armageddon – settlement – Khrushchev climbs down – Pyrrhic victory – exploration of outer space – Russia ahead – Sputniks – First Man in Space – Yuri Gagarin – American moon landings in 1969.

Khrushchev's more pragmatic prosecution of the Cold War and his awareness of 'mutual destruction' led to some lessening of tension. It was, however, always under pressure from 'hard-liners' in the Kremlin and therefore ready for belligerence, as for example when in 1960 an American U2 spy plane was shot down and he made a major issue of it, walking out of a summit meeting angrily when President Eisenhower refused to apologise for it, maintaining that the U2 was a weather plane which had strayed off course (all too easily disproved).[28] Soon afterwards when he met the newly elected youthful American president, John F. Kennedy, he was particularly offensive to test his nerve.[29]

Kennedy, at forty-three the youngest of US presidents, was to inherit a hornets' nest. Crises were looming in different parts of the world. Of these the most pressing at first was in Berlin from where Khrushchev was again attempting to oust the Western Allies. He had once described Berlin as 'a fishbone in the gullet'.[30] It had always been objectionable to have this western capitalist enclave in the middle of communist East Germany. This was especially the case as West Berlin had become conspicuously more prosperous than East Berlin, resulting in a constant stream of refugees pouring across the border. It was reckoned that since 1945 the number of refugees amounted to about two million. This was not only a bad advertisement for communism but also a serious loss to the economy of East Germany as many of the refugees were skilled workers.

The Potsdam Agreement at the end of the Second World War gave the Western powers a legal right to be in Berlin, and this had been confirmed by the Berlin Airlift. However, in a speech in 1958 Khrushchev declared bluntly that it was time this situation came to an end: all occupying powers should leave Berlin and the city become part of the German Democratic Republic. He added that if this had not taken place in six months Russia would sign a separate treaty with East Germany, handing over East Berlin and control of all access routes into the city. He indicated as well that if any dispute about these with the West should arise the Democratic

28 U2s had been carrying out such missions for some time out of reach of anti-aircraft, and Russians had not complained too strongly as it would have meant an admission of superior American technology.

29 Kennedy said later that 'he just beat hell out of me'.

30 More crudely he said that Berlin was 'the testicle of the West and every time I want to make it scream I squeeze on Berlin'.

Republic as a member of the Warsaw Pact would be entitled to help from all other members. This was dynamite, amounting virtually to a declaration of war. It meant that West Berlin would become completely isolated and could no longer exist, an airlift being no longer possible owing to the great increase in population and prosperity of the city. This would be a momentous blow to the prestige of the Western Alliance. There followed a war of nerves in which Khrushchev blew hot and cold; at times reasonably calm and level-headed, but he could not afford to be too accommodating. As the crisis intensified the number of refugees grew ever larger. In the month of July 1961 it was estimated that there were as many as 30,000.

East Germany was clearly losing the battle for 'the hearts and minds' of the German people, and this could not be allowed to continue. In August 1961 with Russian consent the East German government sealed off all entrances into Berlin except for a few official checkpoints and ordered a wall to be constructed along the frontier – 150 miles long, six feet tall, covered in barbed wire and concrete. This monstrosity made escape to the West almost impossible, anyone attempting it being shot at sight. However, daunting though it might be, it was a glaring example of the inadequacy of East Germany in that it had to imprison its citizens behind a horror such as this. For a time, however, it did ease tension and averted a major crisis.

A more dangerous and potentially calamitous crisis was to occur in a different part of the world. After becoming Cuba's dictator in 1959 Fidel Castro had at first been out to show that he was no communist, but when he nationalised land and set up communist style farm cooperatives and became too friendly with communist regimes, the US government took fright and banned the purchase of Cuban sugar, the staple crop of the country on which its economy depended. This did not, however, bring Castro to his knees but drove him deeper into the communist fold, and Khrushchev, seeing the possibility of a Russian satellite off the coast of America, undertook to buy Cuba's sugar and prop up its economy with other commercial aid. This gave rise to panic in some parts of America, and plots were hatched to bring Castro down, the most notorious of which was the disastrous episode of the Bay of Pigs in which a band of discontented Cuban exiles with American backing set out to invade the island, but were soon rounded up and wiped out.[31]

This encouraged Khrushchev to send more military aid to Cuba including the establishment of missile bases. When these were discovered by American spy planes in 1962 it precipitated the most perilous crisis in the Cold War. For if these bases, only ninety miles from the American mainland, were allowed to be completed, every city in the Western hemisphere would be exposed to nuclear attack. President Kennedy decided at once that they could not be tolerated, but how were they to be prevented without setting off a nuclear war?

Kennedy took firm measures, announcing on 22 October that US forces would invade Cuba on 30 October, if the bases had not been removed. He also said that Cuba would be put into 'quarantine', and no ships carrying war supplies would be allowed to land. For a week the situation was tense as the world hovered on the brink of Armageddon; but Kennedy had been at pains not to drive Khrushchev into a corner, leaving him room to negotiate and back down without too much loss of face; and in the end that is what happened. Khrushchev gave way and all bases were removed; but in return Kennedy

31 This venture had been initiated at the end of Eisenhower's presidency. President Kennedy did not like it, but felt bound to let it go on. He should, though, have ensured that it was well organised enough to be successful. If it had been, the history of the Cold War might have been different.

agreed to the withdrawal of US bases in Turkey and gave an undertaking that Cuba would not be invaded by the United States. This was significant. Castro's position was guaranteed, and he was to remain dictator of Cuba for another twenty-five years, stirring up undercover discord throughout the Caribbean and Central and South America. Although economically weak he was able to maintain a standing army which was to be found in the world's trouble spots, even in Africa. It was thus for Kennedy in the nature of a Pyrrhic victory.[32]

Another difficult situation confronting Kennedy on his accession was that of outer space. At that time the Russians were still behind America as regards nuclear weapons; but in the exploration of space they were ahead. On 4 October 1957 they launched Sputnik 1 into space which circled the globe in ninety-five minutes. A month later they sent Sputnik 2 with a dog on board, Laika, who stood no chance of survival but was to win a place in history as the first living creature to go into outer space. Meanwhile American space projects were lagging behind; there was a disaster in December 1957 when the first American space vehicle, the Vanguard, blew up on its launching platform. Three months later a successful launch was made, but the Russians were to maintain their lead for some time, and on 12 April 1961 they achieved the historic feat of sending the first man into space. Yuri Gagarin, aged twenty-seven at the time, had been born on a collective farm in circumstances of hardship. He was to qualify as a test pilot and then specially trained for this mission. He was to make one circuit of the Earth in one hour forty-eight minutes. This feat was publicised widely and loudly by Khrushchev, and Gagarin was paraded proudly before the world. This had an

32 One in which the victor's losses were as great as those of the defeated. Named after Pyrrhus, King of Epirus, who defeated the Romans in a battle in 279 BC.

electric effect on Americans who were spurred into frantic activity, and Kennedy made a rousing speech in which he called for a landing on the Moon within ten years. This was achieved regardless of the cost, which was immense, on 16 July 1969 when Neil Armstrong and Edwin (Buzz) Aldrin set foot on the Moon in the Sea of Tranquillity and with Michael Collins made a safe return into the Pacific, no more than thirty seconds behind schedule.

CHAPTER TEN

VIETNAM

French in Indo-China – war of eight years – Dien Bien Phu – French withdraw – Vietnam divided into north and south – President Kennedy's pledge – de Gaulle's warning – ever more troops needed – Johnson's dilemma – press campaign in United States – violent abuse – retirement of Johnson – Nixon president – total US withdrawal – humiliating defeat – South East Asia overrun by communism – Laos, Cambodia – Khmer Rouge in Cambodia – US more wary of foreign involvement.

By far the most gruelling problem confronting Kennedy and one of the most acute in American history was Vietnam. Only a few weeks after the surrender of Japan in 1945, the revolutionary communist leader, Ho Chi Minh, declared Vietnam's independence from French rule; but the French were convinced that if France was to be re-established as a world power it needed colonies and Indo-China, comprising Vietnam, Laos and Cambodia, had to be regained at all costs. A bitter and barbaric war was then to ensue; for eight years the finest French regiments, including the Foreign Legion, were to fight it out against a ragged, underfed army of peasant farmers, and were not to prevail. This was a triumph of will. Napoleon had once declared that in war moral considerations account for three quarters and the balance of actual forces for only one quarter. Throughout those eight years, the Vietnamese under Võ Nguyên Giáp, a military leader of genius, were to fight with total dedication having no other thought than total victory. The French, on the other hand, had an instinctive feeling that they were fighting a losing battle, in spite of much help in weaponry and other supplies from America. Usually President Eisenhower favoured nationalists rather than colonialists, but in this case he did not want to see communism spreading throughout South East Asia and he needed French support in Europe. In 1954, however, after a major disaster at Dien Bien Phu where a large force surrendered, the French had to agree to leave Indo-China. The war had cost them 93,000 dead.

At an international conference in Geneva in 1954, attended by foreign ministers of Britain, France, America, Russia and communist China, it was agreed that Vietnam should be divided in two along the 17th line of latitude, the north under a communist regime and the south with a democracy. In the following years there was constant rivalry and hostility between them, with the north under the dynamic leadership of Ho Chi Minh gaining the upper hand. It had an army of experienced and dedicated guerrillas ready for a fight, and there was too a 'fifth column'[33] inside South Vietnam known as Viet Cong, lying low during the day and

33 A term said to have originated during the Spanish Civil War denoting an enemy within.

emerging at night to take part in a raid or an ambush, and then disappearing into the countryside.

In his inaugural address in 1961 President Kennedy in ringing tones declared that freedom throughout the world was in danger, that his generation had been given the role of defending freedom and that 'Americans would pay any price, bear any burden, meet any hardship, support any friend to ensure the survival of liberty.' Brave words but fateful.

Kennedy became convinced that the country most in need of support was South Vietnam. Before he came to office the United States had been sending aid including a number of 'advisors' and he soon decided that there should be more of these and there should also be a contingent of troops. This despite a warning from General de Gaulle: 'I prophesy,' he told him, 'that you will sink step by step into a bottomless military and political quagmire.' And it soon became evident that this was indeed the case as more and more troops with air support were needed.

After Kennedy's assassination the new president, Lyndon Johnson, a tough, determined Texan, was faced with a crucial decision. Should he fight the war to a bitter end? Or should he pull out? Whichever way he was a loser. If the former he would have on his hands a long, desperate and unpopular struggle. If the latter he would be charged with weakness and cowardice and the loss of South East Asia to communism. His decision was an uneasy compromise – a war of containment rather than conquest. He would not bring to bear the full force of American power. He would be restrained by moral considerations. He seemed at times to be looking for peace rather than war while Ho Chi Minh was unremitting in his determination to dominate the whole Vietnamese peninsula.

Deadlock seemed to have been reached: it became a war of attrition, which neither side could win. But the situation in the south was deteriorating. President Ngo Dinh Diem was

US soldiers lift wounded Viet Cong
prisoner onto helicopter, 1968.

assassinated in 1963, possibly with American connivance as he was regarded by many as a ruthless and unpopular dictator; but his successors were to prove weaker and less resolute. In spite of overwhelming American fire power the North Vietnamese continued to prevail. It was found that wars could not be won by aerial bombardment alone. At the same time there was a wave of opposition to the war in the United States. Elements of the press mounted a vitriolic campaign against it, showing pictures of its alleged horrors – Flying Fortresses bombing Vietnamese villages and setting fire to the countryside with napalm and pathetic infants dying in agony. Some of this was fallacious and the protestors were a minority but they were active and vociferous. Johnson was assailed with screaming abuse[34] and partly because of this and partly because of the failure of the war he decided not to stand for re-election as president in 1968.

There was a further reason for his standing down as in America Johnson had been pursuing his aim of a 'Great Society' with extensive measures promoting reforms in such matters as housing, health, education and civil rights. These had been highly expensive and in addition to the huge sums spent on the Vietnamese war had put a great strain on the US economy. America might be the richest country in the world but there were limits on what it could afford and by 1965 it was near to crisis.

In 1967 Johnson was succeeded as president by Richard Nixon who decided to pull American troops out of Vietnam and seek an honourable end to the war; but this could not be achieved. Ho Chi Minh was as uncompromising as ever and would settle for nothing less than communist rule over the whole of Vietnam. In 1973 the Paris Peace Accord was

34 Their slogans included 'Ho Chi Minh, the Vietcong are going to win!!' and 'Hey, Hey, LBJ. How many kids have you killed today?'

signed. Vietnam was to remain divided for the time being and US troops would be withdrawn, but fighting between north and south was to continue. In 1975 the North Vietnamese, still receiving massive help from Russia, mounted a strong offensive which the south without American help was unable to resist and on 21 April the war ended with a complete evacuation and Ho Chi Minh supreme over the whole country.

This was America's most humiliating defeat: nearly 46,000 Americans had been killed and none of the American objectives had been achieved. The American climb-down was to have momentous consequences: in Laos, the communist Pathet Lao took over, and in Cambodia all hell was let loose when the fanatical clique known as Khmer Rouge gained power and perpetrated some of the greatest crimes ever against humanity: hordes of citizens from the capital, Phnom Penh, and other cities were driven out into the country where they were put to death brutally or left to die of hunger or exposure. It is estimated that 1,200,000, one fifth of the population, perished.

Another consequence of the Vietnamese debacle was its effect on American popular opinion. The idea of America's coming to the aid of all countries fighting for freedom became less popular. Americans were to become chary of becoming too deeply involved in other countries' wars.

US soldiers in action in Vietnam, 1970.

CHAPTER ELEVEN

A NEW CHINA

Mao revives China regardless of loss of life – successful up to a point – failure of collectivisation of agriculture – historical aversion of Russia and China – present suspicion and mistrust – offended by Khrushchev's denunciation of Stalin – ready for nuclear war – sudden withdrawal of Russian aid – 'Let a hundred flowers bloom' – Great Leap Forward – Little Red Book – continuous revolution – Chiang Ching – Gang of Four – left-wing intellectuals' views of China – Deng Xiaoping – capitalism and communism coexisting – no classless society – Tiananmen Square – subjection of Tibet.

In the years following the Korean war, Mao continued in his course of creating a new China – a mammoth task. After twenty-five years of civil war and fourteen years resisting the Japanese, the condition of China was woeful: roads and railways were in ruin, manufacturing output was half what it had been before the civil war, and inflation was rampant so that money was often invalid. Faced with these conditions Mao was ruthless. The lives of millions were disrupted, millions more would be re-educated or, as he put it, remoulded, and millions more put to death or left to starve. The new China would be based on communism, but Mao was to incorporate many of his own ideas, rewriting the doctrines of Marx and Lenin where it suited him which was to incur increasing hostility from Russia.

He was determined that China should be a major industrial country as soon as possible which needed prodigious efforts on the part of Chinese people, working their hardest with minimum return. To this end he sought to fill everyone with revolutionary zeal and mighty propaganda campaigns were launched exhorting everyone to spare no pains. Ambitious five-year plans were evolved and these had some success notably in coal, electricity and steel (temporarily). But there had been a fatal failure. One of Mao's first acts had been to break up the estates of large landowners and distribute their lands among peasants, but these were inefficient and uncooperative, not being able to afford modern machinery and most of them not interested in new scientific methods so that production was low. And so, as in Russia twenty-five years before, it was decided to 'collectivise' farm holdings, forming them into communes in which everything was owned in common and workers became paid employees; but as in Russia farming communes were unpopular. Farmers wanted their own land and to farm it in their way. They were not prepared to work as hard for a commune nor to take the same amount of care of livestock and machinery that did not belong to them.

It was not likely that there would be friendly relations between Russia and China. Their antagonism lay deep in history. Among Russians there was an instinctive dread of invaders from the East, dating from the fourteenth century when Genghis Khan and his Mongols swept through Russia, leaving behind grisly memorials of towering piles of human skulls. Since then Russians have had an innate fear of 'the yellow hordes of Asia', and in modern times this fear increased with the prospect of a strong united China with an exploding population on their border. At the same time in China there was an underlying suspicion of Russian strength and resentment that Russia still held lands once Chinese which had been occupied by the Russians when China was weak and divided and lay at the mercy of foreigners. At the time of the Russian Revolution there had been an undertaking that these lands would be restored but this had not occurred and did not seem likely to occur.

As has been seen Mao Tse-Tung had had no support from Stalin during the civil war but, nevertheless, he could not but admire him and his ways and was outraged when he was denounced by Khrushchev. He was also shocked when Khrushchev sought better relations with the west; it was not for true communists to compromise with capitalists, he asserted; rather they should be confronting them and seeking to bring them down. He urged the Russians to make greater use of their nuclear capacity, prepared, so it seemed, for a nuclear attack on China with the loss of millions of lives. 'War is war,' he declared. 'The years will pass and we will get to work producing more babies than ever before.' The Russians, however, after coming into close contact with the devastating effect of nuclear weapons, had a more responsible attitude. In waging the Cold War they were prepared to go to the brink but no further.

In 1959 Mao was to step down as head of state, although not to disappear from the scene entirely (remaining as chairman of the Communist Party). In ten years much had been achieved: China was again an independent united country free from foreign interference, its pride and dignity to a large extent restored and significant progress made towards industrialisation. This, however, was to be set back in 1960 when relations with Russia became so tense that Khrushchev suddenly ordered the withdrawal of all Russian aid to China; Russian engineers and other technical experts were recalled, taking their plans and blueprints with them, leaving large-scale projects such as bridges and factories half finished, and machinery idle because there were no spare parts available. Open warfare between the two countries was at times not far off.

Mao was not to remain long on the sidelines. By 1956 he was feeling that his position was insecure. It seemed to him that the Revolution, *his* revolution, was being taken over by people he most dreaded – scientists, technocrats, intellectuals – who were becoming too independent. And so, guilefully, he proclaimed a campaign called lyrically 'Let a hundred flowers bloom' which invited criticism of his regime, but in reality this was a trap for his opponents, of which there were a growing number. Perhaps as many as half a million of these were to be exterminated.

In 1957 Mao announced another Five-Year Plan called 'The Great Leap Forward', but this was to be dogged by disaster – exceptional floods and droughts and low agricultural production combined with Mao's social engineering resulted in three years of famine in which, it is believed, over forty million people starved to death.

One of the consequences of the conflict between Russia and China was that the latter was drawn into closer trade contacts with Western powers to the great benefit of Chinese industry which went ahead faster, as was shown significantly when in 1964 the first Chinese atom bomb was exploded. This progress, however, was not to the liking of Chairman Mao, for it had been obtained at the expense of the things he hated most – large industrial cities, and a rapidly growing middle class of managers and technical experts which come inevitably with industrialisation. More and more he was feeling edged out and not only by industrialists but also by rival politicians and intellectuals who were deviating from the sacred thoughts he had enunciated in his '*Little Red Book*'.[35]

He was concerned that at the age of seventy-two he was to be considered too old for his job and that people were laying plans for a new regime after his death, and perhaps even before it. So he decided that ruthless and dramatic action had to be taken. First to show how fit he still was he went on an alleged nine-mile swim in the River Yangtse. Then in 1965 he loosed on China the Great Proletarian Cultural Revolution, proclaiming that if the purity of communism was to be maintained and China was not to go down the same road as Russia – communism without a cutting edge – the country had to be in a state of 'continuous revolution'. But his real purpose was to expose all of those he looked on as his enemies – the politicians and bourgeois bureaucrats who were usurping his powers – and be rid of them. It was the last desperate bid of an old man to regain lost prestige and power.

In fact the Cultural Revolution was not cultural at all. It was the opposite as most of the main victims were artists, writers and university teachers; and those who carried out the revolution, the so-called Red Guard, were ignorant hooligans, some as young as thirteen or fourteen, who could do little more than vandalise property, shout slogans and assault innocent people. Beautiful monuments were smashed, valuable books burned, shops closed down and plays and other forms of entertainment banned. Eminent artists, writers and university teachers were denounced as 'monsters' and

35 The title of this was 'Quotations from Chairman Mao'. Some 300 million were distributed free.

forced to kneel down and confess their 'faults' on pain of having their hair torn out, and then paraded through the streets wearing dunces' caps and surrounded by screaming youths waving *The Little Red Book*. More humble citizens too were not safe: girls' long 'Western-style' hair was shorn and boys wearing tight trousers had them removed. For three years the people of China were ravaged by these mobs. The consequences of the 'Cultural Revolution' to China were disastrous. Schools and universities had to close down, factories and businesses came to a halt as key workers were taken away to listen to political harangues or take part in demonstrations.

Prominent during the Cultural Revolution was Mao's fourth wife, Chiang Ching, a loose living ex-actress whom Mao had married in 1939 but who for twenty-five years had been kept in the background; in 1964 she was let loose and allowed to run riot with wild ideas about revolutionising Chinese theatre and arts in general. Mao gave her a free hand and there was no stopping her. Gathering together a mixed band of disgruntled actors, writers and artistic hangers-on, she formed a society known as The League of Left-Wing Dramatists who sought to disrupt orthodox productions and replace them with way-out incomprehensible matter which interested no one. During the Cultural Revolution she was in the midst of it at the head of a so-called Gang of Four, urging Red Guards on to ever more atrocities until even Mao called a stop to it so that for a time they parted company.

Mao Tse-Tung died on 27 September 1976 after dominating China for twenty-seven years. He had achieved much: China had been put back on the map, converted from a land of peasant proprietors to an industrial giant and on the way to becoming an even greater one. But this had been achieved at a cost: unaccountable millions had been dispossessed or lost their lives. He had ruled throughout by repression; individual freedom was unknown; people went in fear of their lives.[36] And yet there were foreign visitors, mainly left-wing intellectuals, who looked on China as a dream world and Mao as a wonder. Simone de Beauvoir, French existentialist philosopher, would write that 'life in China today is exceptionally pleasant.' An American theorist said of Mao that when a problem arose Mao invariably responded in a uniquely creative and profoundly ethical way, and the Right Reverend Hewlett Johnson, the Red Dean of Canterbury, as always a mine of disinformation, would write of the greatest mass murderer in history that he had 'an inexpressible look of kindness and sympathy and an obvious preoccupation with the needs of others'.[37] At the time of Mao's death Chiang Ching and the Gang of Four attempted to seize power, but they were suppressed by the Politburo, Chiang was condemned to death and committed suicide in prison.

To become head of state was Hua Kuo-Feng whom Mao had nominated as his successor, but real power was to lie with his deputy, Deng Xiaoping. Deng was a canny operator who had come to the top by keeping a low profile and introducing change inconspicuously. He was to guide China into a new era in which rampant capitalism co-existed with a form of communism. It was clear to him, as to an increasing number, that if China was to become a worldwide industrial power this could only be achieved by means of capitalism. Communist economics got one nowhere. And so capitalist entrepreneurs were allowed great latitude, and many were to become inordinately rich. But Marxist-Leninism was not abandoned; China did not become a classless society and

36 Amazingly the population of China during Mao's rule increased from 550 million to 900 million.

37 Quoted from *History of the Modern World 1917–1980* by Paul Johnson (Weidenfeld and Nicolson, 1982).

the gap between rich and poor was as wide as ever, and the government still relied on repression to stay in power.

In the 1980s, however, it seemed that China was set on more peaceful and open ways. The insanity of the Cultural Revolution of 1965 had subsided, Mao Tse-Tung had died in 1976 and change was being introduced by stealth. But then in the spring of 1989 the communist leaders suddenly took fright and decided that affairs were moving out of their control. When there was a massive demonstration by students in favour of democracy in Tiananmen Square, the forces of law and order were turned out against them ruthlessly. The demonstration was to last seven weeks, and it is believed that more than 3,000 lives were lost, while the police and army were praised for their 'heroic response to the perfidious inhumanity of students.' This was a milestone in Chinese history. For the time being the way to democracy and open government was barred. At the same time in Tibet a popular movement was crushed.

And so China was to remain an alliance between capitalist financiers and political doctrinaires. They rule by repression, allowing no freedom of speech or writing; but capitalists are free to become as rich as they like provided they deliver a great industrial state – a combination which has achieved wonders. But for how long?

CHAPTER TWELVE

DECOLONISATION OF AFRICA

Shameful past history – slave trade – Triangular Trade – Belgian Congo – Leopold II – winds of change – self-government inevitable – French in Algeria – natural riches of Africa – gold, precious stones – ivory – rubber – democracies overturned – one-party states – despotic rulers – strife in Rhodesia – Robert Mugabe until 2017 – apartheid in South Africa – separate development – release of Nelson Mandela – introduction of parliamentary government in 1992.

The Cold War was to extend into Africa. There the record of capitalism was to be seen at its worst. The continent was long regarded by Europeans primarily as a source of slaves to be sold in North and South America. First in this trade had been the Portuguese in Angola and Mozambique in the fifteenth century. British seafarers were to become involved in Elizabethan times in the so-called Triangular Trade, sailing empty vessels from England to West Africa where they would take on board a cargo of slaves purchased usually from African chieftains in exchange for such things as guns and brandy, and then in the dreaded Middle Passage, where the treatment of the slaves was unspeakable, to America where they would sell them. This trade was made illegal in Britain in 1807.[38]

These European traders were concerned only with what they could extort; the welfare of the native population meant nothing to them and Africans were treated with contempt. The worst offender was King Leopold II of Belgium (uncle of Queen Victoria) who in 1885 appropriated a large area in the basin of the River Congo to become known as the Belgian Congo. There natives were murdered or mutilated ruthlessly in order to get what was needed from them. Belgian rule was to last until 1960. The British were not blameless in their colonies but there were some who showed concern for the Africans, although more for their souls than their political rights, and were active in exploring and developing the interior of the continent.

It was argued by many in the first half of the twentieth century that African countries were not ready for self-government and not greatly interested in having it, but this was not the case. In 1958 on a visit to South Africa the British Prime Minister Harold Macmillan, declared: 'the wind of change is blowing through this continent and, whether we like it or not this growth of national consciousness is a political fact.'

When it became accepted that self-government had to come sooner rather than later the process of decolonisation proceeded mostly without undue stress or bloodshed.

38 Slavery itself was abolished in Britain in 1833 and in the United States in 1865. By then European traders were becoming more interested in exploiting Africa's natural riches – gold, precious stones, ivory and rubber (then in great demand for the tyres of the newly developing bicycles).

Crises did arise, particularly in Algeria while the French determination to hold on to their colony to the bitter end nearly caused a civil war in France. There was strife in Rhodesia for a time and for longer in South Africa.

The British hoped that when they left each colony would have a democratic system of government in place similar to their own which would be viable and enduring. But this was expecting too much. In the years that followed independence, parliaments were usually undermined, opposition parties subdued and a one-party state with a despotic ruler set permanently in power. The main British colony in which there was serious dispute was Rhodesia, founded by the English multi-millionaire Cecil Rhodes. For a number of years it was the property of The British South Africa Company, but in 1923 it became a self-governing British colony which meant that it had independence in all matters except foreign affairs and laws relating to the rights of Africans. The white colonists in Rhodesia were strongly aware of being a small minority in the middle of a much larger number of blacks (native Africans) (about 241,000 Europeans and 4.4 million indigenous people). They maintained that they and their forefathers had worked hard and lived dangerously to build up the prosperity of the country which, they thought, would disappear under black rule; but this attitude was becoming increasingly outdated: to most people in Britain and in the rest of the world majority rule was essential.

Various ways were contrived to maintain white rule but these took little account of 'the wind of change' and were doomed. In April 1980 the independent Republic of Zimbabwe was proclaimed by the party of Robert Mugabe who became president, which he was to remain until 2017 (he died in 2019).

The struggle for majority rule was more prolonged and more bitter in South Africa where there was a larger white population than in any other African territory. Parts of the country had originally been settled more than 300 years earlier by the Boers (later also known as Afrikaners) who were mainly of Dutch origin. They were to keep themselves apart when numerous British colonists moved in after Britain had annexed the Cape of Good Hope in 1814 after the Napoleonic Wars. Relations between Boers and Britons were fraught and came to a head with the Boer War (1899–1902) in which the British were eventually victorious. The two groups were united in the Union of South Africa in 1910 and there was unity during both world wars, but soon afterwards the position began to change.

In a general election in 1948 a majority was gained by the Boer Nationalist Party which was determined to maintain white supremacy and imposed on the country the regime known as *apartheid* which involved the separation of white and black races. This was to be enforced ruthlessly: blacks were compelled to live in separate townships (evicted from their present homes where necessary) and sent to separate schools, travelled in separate parts of public transport and used separate public buildings and beaches. In addition blacks had no political rights and their freedom of movement was restricted by 'pass laws' which required them to carry at all times kinds of identity cards saying to which racial group they belonged and which barred them from going into certain areas. At the same time the government took dictatorial powers to suppress riots, put away political opponents and censor the press.

In theory *apartheid* meant 'separate development' and did not involve racial superiority and black subjugation, but it had that effect; black people became second-class citizens where the white population depended on them for labour, and the economy of South Africa would have collapsed without them. Inevitably such a policy caused outrage in the outside world and nowhere more so than in the new Commonwealth of Nations which was growing rapidly as new countries joined after attaining independence.[39] As its essence was that all members were equal regardless of race, it was clearly not the place for South Africa which left the Commonwealth of its own accord in 1961. South Africa subsequently became more and more cut off from the rest of the world. In 1962 the United Nations imposed sanctions on the country, cutting off almost all foreign trade, but for a time, ways were found round the sanctions and they did not have a great effect on the South African economy. More upsetting to many was the country's exclusion from world cultural and sporting events.

By the end of the 1970s it was evident that South Africans could not exist indefinitely in isolation from the rest of the world. A major breakthrough came in 1989 when F.W. de Klerk became president. He was on the more liberal wing of the Nationalist Party and was determined that *apartheid* had to go. He announced the end of it the following year and he released from prison, where he had been for twenty-seven years, Nelson Mandela, the most famous and charismatic of African leaders on whom much was to depend. Nothing now could stop the movement for reform. In 1992 a referendum was held among the white citizens of South Africa which showed that seventy per cent were in favour of ending *apartheid* and the introduction of parliamentary government with one man, one vote. This represented a significant advance for the cause of capitalism.

39 Between 1945 and 1968 the Commonwealth had grown from five members to twenty-eight.

CHAPTER THIRTEEN

NEW ATTITUDES AND BELIEFS

Death of Leonid Brezhnev – Andrei Sakharov – Boris Pasternak – Doctor Zhivago – Alexander Solzhenitsyn – imprisonment – release – One Day in the Life of Ivan Denisovich – influence of Khrushchev – centre of a power struggle – arrested and sent into exile – life in America – disagreements – opposition to materialism – rise of Mikhail Gorbachev – return to Russia – opposition – an anachronism – consumerism too ingrained – permissiveness in Britain – relaxation of moral standards – discontent of youth – Britain stuck in the past – new outlooks.

When Leonid Brezhnev died in 1982 after eighteen years in power, communism seemed as firmly entrenched as ever. The countries of Eastern Europe were still subjugated. Communism had overwhelmed China and nearly all South East Asia; and Russian influence in Africa and the Middle East was expanding. Russia's conventional ground forces were larger than those of both the United States and the Western

Allies, and its nuclear power was almost equal. Inside Russia the position of communist hard-liners seemed secure. They knew on which side their bread was buttered, that their power and prosperity depended on repression and they were against all change. Change, however, was bound to come.

Lively, intelligent minds could not remain in perpetual bondage to orthodox communism. It was intolerable that people could not have ideas of their own. Were they forever to be barred from the great works of art, literature and music of the Western world? Dissidents there were and always would be.

Prominent among these dissidents was Andrei Sakharov, a leading Russian scientist who had had a vital role in the development of Russia's hydrogen bomb.[40] He had been seriously alarmed by its destructive powers and had been calling for such measures as unilateral disarmament, world government and intellectual freedom. In 1975 he had been awarded a Nobel Peace Prize but his views were not in accord with those of the Politburo which forbade him to receive the prize and sentenced him to exile in the 'closed city' of Gorki from 1980 to 1986 when he was released by order of Mikhail Gorbachev.

Another influential dissident was Boris Pasternak from a wealthy Jewish family in Moscow. His original interests had been music and poetry from which at first he could only earn a living by declaiming it in bars and cafés. Later in life he had a compulsion to write something of deep social significance. He later described *Doctor Zhivago* as 'a novel-parable concerned with the need of the human soul to strive for higher sources of spiritual wealth.' 'During the short period of time we live in the world,' he wrote, 'we have to understand our attitude toward existence, and our place in the

40 The first of these had been set off in 1953.

universe. Otherwise life is meaningless. This, as I understand it, means a rejection of the nineteenth-century materialistic world view and a resurrection of our interior life and of religion.' *Doctor Zhivago* was to become world famous as a book and a film; but it was not popular in the Kremlin where it was thought to lack 'social realism and be concerned with welfare of the individual rather than of society' and contained hostility to Stalinist communism. It was, however, to win a Nobel Prize for Literature in 1958. Pasternak died two years later at the age of seventy.

The most influential dissident was Alexander Solzhenitsyn, born in 1918, the son of an officer in the Tsarist army who had been killed in a hunting accident. He was brought up by his mother in conditions of penury and insecurity as in 1918 revolutionary fever was at its height and anyone with royalist connections was at the mercy of revolutionary fanatics.

After the German invasion of Russia in 1941 Solzhenitsyn joined the Russian army in which he served with distinction, rising to the rank of captain with two citations for courage and competence. But in 1945 a letter of his was discovered with criticisms of Stalin and Stalinism. For this he was arrested and after a mockery of a trial sentenced to eight years' imprisonment which he was to serve in full. In the course of this he came close to death during an operation for cancer which he was to describe as the most important and defining moment of his life when he became converted to Christianity. He also had a strong urge to write, but as the authorities disapproved of writing he had to do this in secret on scraps of paper and then memorise what he had written. Altogether he was to commit to memory some 12,000 lines – the beginnings of momentous works of literature.

On 13 February 1956 after four years in the army and eight in prison followed shortly afterwards by the death of

Stalin he was free to write and words came pouring from him. He had especially in mind a work which would bring home to Russian people and to the world how monstrously unjust and inhuman was the treatment of prisoners in forced labour camps, a brave thing to do as the KGB would be watching and he might be back in prison. However, he was determined to do it and in a few weeks he had completed *One Day in the Life of Ivan Denisovich*, a book of historic importance.

It had a mixed reception at the time, strongly condemned in some quarters but approved by Khrushchev who thought it might add weight to his anti-Stalin campaign. Solzhenitsyn was then to live dangerously although somewhat less so after he was awarded the Nobel Prize for Literature in 1970. He continued to write outspokenly and managed to survive until it became known that he was writing a history of the KGB with no holds barred. The KGB then took action: he was arrested and sent into exile with his wife and three sons, first to Switzerland and then to the United States. In America he was to find himself not wholly welcome. At the time the mood was one of détente. It was widely remarked that he was not invited to the White House. He was also at variance with the American public because of the spread of materialism.[41] For him life without spiritual values was empty and purposeless. A consequence of these differences was that Solzhenitsyn and his family withdrew to a fastness in Vermont where he distanced himself from outsiders and devoted himself to writing. His books, although banned in Russia, had wide circulation in other countries, usually being translated into over thirty languages.

Solzhenitsyn's love of Russia was always deep within him and he was convinced that he was destined to return

41 Defined by the Oxford Dictionary as 'a strong interest in possessions and physical comfort rather than spiritual values'.

there. In the mid-1980s it seemed that the time for this might be imminent with the arrival on the scene of Mikhail Gorbachev and the subsequent collapse of communism, but it was not until 1994 at the age of seventy-six that he made his return; and in Moscow he was to have a mixed reception. There were those who looked on him as an apostle of truth and enlightenment, but there were others who regarded him as something of an anachronism. Communism was by then virtually dead, but it was being replaced by materialism which Solzhenitsyn considered almost as bad; acquisitiveness and gratification of every desire without moral considerations he thought to be a living death. He could not but be aware of this apathy and suspected that he could not prevail against it. He might have had a significant role in overcoming fascism and communism, but materialism (otherwise consumerism) was too deeply ingrained. He continued to write voluminously and was to live until 2008, just short of his ninetieth birthday.

In Britain, as in Russia, new attitudes were spreading. In the sixties and seventies youth was becoming restless and rebellious. Since the war British people had had free education, free medical care and other social benefits, but there was a feeling among the younger generation that the country had not moved with the times and was stuck in the past. There was too much convention and complacency and not enough looking forward into a brave new world. This was taken to heart by some of the older generation and there were a number of changes in ways of life: subjects which had once been taboo in polite society were brought into the open and talked about freely. There was a general feeling that, rightly or wrongly, greater freedom would bring greater contentment and there were significant reforms: the death penalty was abolished, divorce became easier, contraception more widely practised and homosexuality between consenting adults legalised. The Church of England became more flexible and open to argument; its precepts on sexuality and the sanctity of family life were modified and consideration was given to such matters as the ordination of women and unisexual marriages.

Controversy was at times to be heated and occasionally violent; some young people seemed to delight in angry protests and rousing demonstrations just for the sake of them. Cynicism and mockery seemed to be the order of the day. Amid the clamour and strife the lives of ordinary citizens remained orderly and routine for them – 'the trivial task and the common round'.[42] Regularity and sameness came naturally to some, but there were unquiet souls yearning for something more adventurous and heroic – more in line with Byron and Garibaldi than home-grown do-gooders like Lord Beveridge.[43] In Britain there were no dangerous subversive groups like the Baader-Meinhof gang in Germany or the Red Brigade in Italy. Most young people were more interested in their university degrees and subsequent careers, and were to find that their elders were not always narrow-minded bigots and sometimes even founts of wisdom.

42 The English Hymnal.

43 British economist whose report during the war on social security ('from the cradle to the grave') is regarded by many as the foundation of the welfare state.

CHAPTER FOURTEEN

TURN OF THE TIDE

Ascendancy of communism declines – invasion of Afghanistan – significance of Russian failure – election of Ronald Reagan – his aggressiveness – accession of Mikhail Gorbachev – glasnost and perestroika – failure of collectivised agriculture – Russian industry outstripped by capitalism – need for economic and political change – Gorbachev cautious – powers of Old Guard – false alarms in Kremlin – fears of pre-emptive strikes – Able Archer – modification of Reagan – talks on arms control – START – meeting between Gorbachev and Thatcher – mutual appreciation – influence of Oleg Gordievsky – information as double agent – Gordievsky and Philby contrasted – Gorbachev's achievements – nearly overthrown by a coup in 1991 – saved by Yeltsin – Yeltsin humiliates him in Parliament – he retires – Yeltsin as president – survival of communism into twenty-first century.

The ascendancy of communism in parts of the world during the 1970s was not to last long in the 1980s. It began in 1979 when the Russians made the fatal mistake of invading Afghanistan. In the past other countries, including Britain, had attempted this and regretted it. Invasions had come to nothing. Afghanistan, as the Russians eventually discovered, proved unconquerable. A war was to drag on for nearly ten years, and when the Russians finally withdrew it was for them a disaster comparable to the American defeat in Vietnam. It was the first time that Stalinist communism had been forced to retreat, and the significance of this was not lost on other communist countries. It was a sign that the Soviet Union might no longer be willing to support them with armed forces as they had done in the past in order to subdue anti-communist movements.

In 1980 a new situation arose when Ronald Reagan, a one-time film actor and governor of California, was elected president of the United States. He announced that he was going to give priority, regardless of cost, to gaining military superiority over all potential enemies. And this he was in a position to do. In furtherance of his belligerent stance he also gave utterance to rhetorical language, describing the Soviet Union as 'an evil empire', and his aim was 'to leave Marxist-Leninism in an ash heap of history.' He forged ahead with developing nuclear weapons to give America a lead over Russia and initiated the Strategic Defense Initiative (nicknamed Star Wars) to enable America to counter Russia's nuclear arsenal.

When Brezhnev died in 1982 he was succeeded by sixty-eight-year-old Yuri Andropov, head of the KGB, who was followed two years later by Konstantin Chernenko, even older and virtually moribund who died after a year. Then at last a younger man came to the fore in 1985 when Mikhail Gorbachev, son of a combine harvester operator, became general secretary of the Communist Party at the age of fifty-four, bringing glasnost (openness) and perestroika (reconstruction). A communist of a different hue, his appointment marked a new era in Russian and world history. The problems facing him were daunting, principally that of agriculture, run by collectivised farms so ineffectively that the Soviet Union with some of the best farmlands in Europe was having to rely on huge imports of grain mainly from the United States and Canada to avoid mass starvation.

Russian industry too was not keeping pace with Western countries; its rate of growth was one third that of the United States and one quarter that of Japan. Roads, railways, housing, hospitals and all public services (known collectively as 'infrastructure') were running down and in urgent need of repair and replacement. Generally the standard of living of the average Russian was one quarter that of the average American and markedly lower than that of most Europeans. This being the case, Russia was in no condition to take on the United States in a new round of the arms race. If it did it must lose. It was clear to Gorbachev that basic changes were necessary in the Soviet Union, particularly in the economy, and that these changes had to involve a move away from communism and rigid central control towards a free market and private enterprise. He must also have realised that economic changes would result inevitably in political changes. To bring about the modernisation of Russian industry massive help would be needed from the West and this would only be forthcoming if there were radical changes in the Soviet Union's repressive domestic regime. For some time the Western powers had been urging the Soviet government to give more respect to human rights in such matters as freedom of speech and religion and the granting of visas to Soviet citizens wishing to emigrate or travel abroad, but in the Brezhnev era these had fallen on deaf ears. At a conference in Helsinki in 1975, attended

Mikhail Gorbachev and his wife Raisa with
British Prime Minister Margaret Thatcher in the Kremlin
(undated but possibly on her visit to Moscow in 1987).

by thirty-five countries, Russia had agreed to acknowledge basic human rights, but it soon became apparent that this was deceptive and harsh punishments were still being meted out to anyone speaking on behalf of them.

In his first years in office Gorbachev talked much of the need for change but had to act cautiously. The powers of the Old Guard, still intent on orthodoxy and Marxist-Leninism, remained formidable. He himself was to stay in broad support of communism, bound by some of its rigours and deceptions. He made only small movements towards a free market and private enterprise: some land was allowed to be farmed privately and a few industries were released from central control; but the immediate consequences of these changes were not prominent. His slowness to act caused some mistrust abroad. It was noted that there had been no reductions in Russia's armed forces. Was his liberalisation just a ploy to gain time for a Russian recovery and the survival of communism? These fears were to subside, however, with the later agreements on arms control.

Reagan's initial aggression was to have its dangers. In the 1970s when nuclear forces of East and West were approximately equal it was generally accepted that a nuclear war would bring total ruin to both victors and vanquished, known as 'mutually assured destruction.' This brought about a near stalemate with both sides holding back, but when America drew ahead in the arms race and Reagan spoke out offensively it gave rise to suspicion. In 1981 Andropov, then head of the KGB, became convinced that the United States was planning to launch a pre-emptive nuclear strike to obliterate the Soviet Union. This was a false alarm as no such plan existed but Andropov was obsessed by it and overreacted. In what became known as Operation RYAN Russian forces throughout the world – submarines, missile sites, fully charged warheads – were put on alert as were all KGB agents abroad who were told to find evidence of an American plan of destruction. They were told to note all irregularities, even such trivial matters as increased electric light in government offices and overfull car parks. They could find nothing of significance because it did not exist, but in order to satisfy their boss they felt bound to produce something. This led to a highly dangerous febrile state with nerves on edge and wrong conclusions being drawn. US leaders thought the scare so ridiculous that it could be ignored, but in this they were mistaken. It existed and did not immediately go away.

It was enhanced when in November 1983 a Soviet fighter aircraft shot down a Korean airliner which had strayed into Soviet air space, killing all 269 passengers and crew. This led to an angry exchange, Reagan describing the incident as 'an act of barbarism and inhuman brutality'; and the Kremlin claiming that the airliner was a spy plane that had violated Soviet air space in a criminal provocation by the United States. A more critical event was a military exercise mounted by the United States and NATO forces in 1983 known as 'Able Archer'. This was to rehearse manoeuvres in the event of an invasion by Warsaw Pact countries. It was entirely simulated and no nuclear weapons were involved, but alarmists in the Kremlin saw it as a preparation for a nuclear first strike. A tense and dangerous situation developed that came close to setting off declaration of war. Of this the general public in Europe and America was unaware, but those in the know recognised that it was the nearest to a nuclear apocalypse since the Cuban crisis of 1962. The atmosphere was to subside but it had had a profound effect on some, notably President Reagan to whom it was an eye-opener; he was shocked by how close it had come to holocaust, and he thought this was liable to occur again in the Cold War should a moment of panic or illusion lead someone to take a fatal

Ronald Reagan, 40th President of the United States, and Mikhail Gorbachev, General Secretary of the Communist Party of the Soviet Union (undated but presumably after 1985).

step. So he modified his attitude, lowering the tone of his rhetoric and preparing for talks on arms control.

In 1981, in the Stockholm Accord, a conference of thirty-five nations had already agreed to give advance notice of NATO and Warsaw Pact troop movements to reduce the risk of accidental conflict. In 1982, negotiations started between America and Russia that eventually led to Strategic Arms Reduction Talks (which came to be known as START I) aimed at limiting medium and short-range missiles. Those talks were concluded in 1987, although the treaty was not signed until 1991 and came into effect only in 1994.

This drawing together of the two powers was enhanced by a meeting in 1984 between Mikhail Gorbachev, not yet head of state but the rising star of the Communist Party, and the British prime minister, Margaret Thatcher, then at the height of her fame after the British victory in the Falkland Islands in 1982 and always a virulent and outspoken opponent of communism. It was expected that they might clash vociferously, but in the event they took to each other and, though differing widely and arguing forcefully, there was mutual appreciation, Mrs Thatcher declaring at the end that Gorbachev was a man with whom she could do business; no mean compliment from her.

In her talks with Gorbachev Mrs Thatcher had guidance and elucidation from an unlikely source. Oleg Gordievsky was a Russian double agent who for nine years had been supplying secret information to MI6. He was a long-serving KGB officer and originally a fully indoctrinated communist but had become disillusioned. The ways of communist despotism became intolerable to him. He was appalled by some of the execrable deeds of the KGB and frustrated by the restrictions imposed on him. He could not abide being disallowed his own opinions and the suppression of his conscience – it was too much for an independent spirit.

He had, however, shown himself a capable KGB officer and in 1983 was appointed chief of political intelligence in the Russian Embassy in London. This meant that during Gorbachev's visit he had access to secret information from both the KGB and MI6; both sides were to be briefed by him. Feeling strongly that the Cold War should be brought to an end, he took it upon himself to create the best atmosphere for leaders to communicate with each other. And so he provided to MI6 not only military details but also background material such as current opinions and traits of Russian leaders, what was troubling them most and how they should be approached. At the same time he told the KGB of the trends of President Reagan and others, on which matters they were adamant and those where they might be prepared to make concessions, and how tactlessness and misapprehension might be avoided. His reports to MI6 were forwarded to Mrs Thatcher who sent them on to President Reagan who found them invaluable. They were to lay the grounds for future conferences with Gorbachev including three summits in 1986.

As a double agent Gordievsky is to be contrasted with Kim Philby. Both were men of great courage and resourcefulness but differed widely on fundamentals. Philby's actions aggravated and prolonged the Cold War, causing extensive loss of life and ending in failure and disaster. Gordievsky on the other hand had a significant role in ending the Cold War with little bloodshed.

Gorbachev was to make his mark on history. Within Russia, as has been seen, he had to be cautious but he achieved much. Glasnost brought more freedom of speech and opinions, many political prisoners were set free, the activities of the KGB were restricted and he had overseen the establishment of a new type of Russian parliament, still very different from those of the West (of 2,250 seats only 395 were freely elected), but a distinct advance on the old Supreme

Soviet. He had also made a significant contribution to the subsiding of the Cold War. Perhaps most important of all, as will be seen, was his allowance of increased independence to the Russian satellites in Eastern Europe.

Much as Gorbachev had achieved, however, it was not enough. In one crucial matter he had failed: perestroika had not brought significant prosperity. The standard of living of Russian people had hardly improved. According to the hard-liners this was because of the changes he had introduced, and they were urging a return to the ways of the Brezhnev era. In August 1991 they planned a coup to overthrow him, which might have succeeded as it was backed by the defence minister, the minister of the interior and the head of the KGB. It was, however, to come to nothing as there were enough of those who believed that what was needed was more, not less, movement towards a free economy, and they were to find a dynamic and charismatic leader. It was a quirk of fate that the bloodless transition in Russia from communism to capitalism was brought about mainly by Boris Yeltsin – rough and ready, dissolute and a drunkard. He took the lead in thwarting the plot of the Old Guard, at one time mounting a tank to urge the crowds to reject it. His day had come. Having laid low the conspirators he turned his attention to Gorbachev whom he was determined to displace. He was in a strong position to do so as in 1991 he had been elected president of the Russian Republic.[44] It was he who had saved Gorbachev from the Old Guard and he was to rub it in. In Parliament he compelled Gorbachev against his will to read out a list of his ministers who had taken part in the coup against him. Temporarily Gorbachev remained in office, but his time was running out. He had to agree to the granting of complete independence

44 The largest of the republics making up the Soviet Union – three quarters of the area and nearly half of the population.

of the Baltic states of Estonia, Latvia and Lithuania and to the Warsaw Pact being disbanded; and he could only stand by while Yeltsin signed a decree dissolving the Communist Party in the Russian Republic, an example soon followed by other republics who sought independence. Gorbachev had to accept that for him it was the end and in December 1991 he retired into private life.

Communism was not to die down completely in the twenty-first century. Communist ideology may have lapsed, but communist ways and means are still evident. Repression in China and Russia is still rife. Freedom to accumulate wealth is allowed but not freedom of conscience. Vladimir Putin, who became president of the Russian Federation in 2000, had risen from the ranks of the KGB and has since been as aggressive and intolerant as any communist dictator – expansionist and ready to exploit weaknesses among his neighbours.

In China Marxist-Leninism is still held in reverence, but it is not allowed to stand in the way of economic prosperity. It remains to be seen how long such a combination survives.

CHAPTER FIFTEEN

LIBERATION OF EAST EUROPE

Communism in Poland – Pope John Paul II – Solidarity – Lech Walesa – decline of communism in Hungary – Hungarian Democratic Forum — revival of communism in Czechoslovakia – Vaclav Havel as president – Socialist Republic under Nicolae Ceausescu for twenty-two years – Ceausescu executed – National Salvation Front – German Democratic Republic under Erich Honecker – Stasi helpless without backing of Russian army – reunification of West and East Germany in 1990 – civil war in Yugoslavia – dominance of Serbia – Serbian invasion of Croatia – ethnic cleansing – UN intervention in difficulty – in the Hague Serbian leaders charged with genocide.

One of Gorbachev's principal achievements in office lay in the abandonment of support for subject communist regimes abroad. Several were to gain independence, notably in 1989, the bicentenary of the French Revolution.

In Poland there had always been antipathy to communism centred mainly around the Roman Catholic Church; and this had been stimulated when in 1978 Cardinal Karol Wojtyla was elected Pope John Paul II, the first non-Italian pope since 1522 and the youngest for more than a century. Charismatic and eloquent, he was to have wide influence.

In 1980 an independent self-governing trade union was founded in Gdansk (formerly Danzig) under the leadership of Lech Walesa, an electrician and shipyard worker. Known as Solidarity, it gained wide popular support, so much so that it was suppressed by the communist Polish government and Walesa for a time was imprisoned; but in 1989 following a public outcry the government felt obliged to come to an agreement with Solidarity whereby the movement was legalised, greater freedom of speech allowed and partially free elections were promised for ten months later. In these most seats were reserved for communists but all those freely elected were gained by Solidarity supporters which led to the resignation of the communist government and the establishment two months later of the first non-communist government in Eastern Europe. Walesa was elected president in the following year.

In 1988 a moderate communist government was allowed in Hungary, which hoped to maintain communist ascendancy by granting a few liberal reforms. It was, however, to discover that it had stirred up forces it could not control; the more reforms it granted the more were demanded and in 1989 the government was compelled to allow the formation of a non-communist opposition so that no single party would ever again have sole control of the government. From then on the reform movement gathered momentum: more freedom was allowed to religious groups and to the press; and in 1990 a democratic government known as the Hungarian Democratic Forum was freely elected and the Communist Party dissolved, and Hungary became a member of the Council of Europe.

In Czechoslovakia freedom and democracy had always been latent. Since the crushing of the so-called 'Prague Spring' in 1968 the country had been ruled by hard-line communists, but following the successful democratic movements in Poland and Hungary reform was gathering strength. In November 1989 after widespread riots and a refusal of military intervention from Gorbachev the communist government was compelled to resign and was replaced by a non-communist administration under the playwright Vaclav Havel who was elected president five months later.

No Eastern European state suffered so much under communism as Romania. After the abdication of King Michael in 1947, the country had been ruled by a People's Republic, later changed to a Socialist Republic, which was to become dominated by Nicolae Ceausescu, a ruthless tyrant who was in office for twenty-two years. During that time, his despotic ways and 'social engineering', which involved the destruction of some 8,000 rural villages and their replacement by 'agro-industrial complexes' meant that the standard of living of Romanians became the lowest in Europe. Ceausescu was finally brought down on Christmas Day 1989 when he was captured and summarily shot along with his equally offensive wife. He was succeeded for a time by a partly communist group known as The National Salvation Front which won an overall majority in a general election in 1990.

In the German Democratic Republic (GDR) communism had its tightest hold. An uprising in 1953 was subdued by Russian tanks, and from 1971 the country had been held in subjection by the iron rule of Erich Honecker backed by Russian military forces and a ruthlessly efficient secret service known as Stasi. The iron rule, however, had its flaws: until the construction of the Berlin Wall it could not prevent the ever-increasing flow of refugees from East Germany to the West, and could only be sustained by the

Russian army. When that army was removed by Gorbachev in 1989 the GDR was doomed, its fate expedited by events in other East European countries. In October 1989 Honecker was compelled to resign and this was a signal for increased anti-communist activities. A new communist government held office for a time but it grew ever weaker and had to sit by amid general rejoicing while the hated Berlin Wall was demolished, giving free access to the West. At the same time non-communists were admitted into the government and a free election promised. When this occurred in March 1990 there were large majorities for anti-communist parties and the question of the reunification of the two Germanys arose. There were serious difficulties owing to the preponderant wealth of West Germany and how far the two states had grown apart since the end of the Second World War, but these were overcome and agreement reached. On 3 October 1990 Germany was once again fully reunited.

On the whole the transition from communism to democracy in Eastern Europe occurred with little bloodshed, but there was an exception to this in Yugoslavia where there was bitter fighting. After the First World War Yugoslavia was put together as a country consisting of seven South Slav states (Serbia, Croatia, Slovenia, Montenegro, Bosnia, Herzegovina and Macedonia). But although they were ethnically similar the states differed widely in religion and culture[45] and the union was always fragile. Since the Second World War the country had been held together by communism and the forceful character of its president, Marshal Tito. When he died in 1984 the country showed signs of breaking up. The largest and most powerful of the seven states was Serbia and when in 1989 President Milosevic, the communist leader, proclaimed a policy of Greater Serbia it

45 The religion of Serbia was mainly Christian Orthodox, that of Croatia and Slovenia Roman Catholic and that of Bosnia Roman Catholic with Orthodox and Muslim minorities.

caused alarm in the other states who feared Serbian domination and the retention of unwanted communism.

In June 1991 Slovenia and Croatia declared their independence, but this Serbia would not accept, especially in the case of Croatia where some half million Serbs were living. And so the Yugoslav army, predominantly Serbian, was sent into Croatia to 'safeguard' the Serbs living there and to prevent the creation of a separate Croatian state. That was where most of the initial fighting took place. Worse, however, was to occur in Bosnia where there was a Muslim minority, and differences between the various groups were most acute with Serb irregular troops putting into practice a fearsome policy which came to be known as 'ethnic cleansing' involving torture, massacres and other horrors. This caused outcries from foreign countries and calls for intervention, but there were difficulties about this. The United Nations sent peacekeeping troops to attempt to separate the opposing forces but with only limited success. By December 1992 the Serbs had occupied seventy per cent of Bosnia and in spite of persistent efforts by United Nations mediators a settlement acceptable to all parties could not be found.

In 1993 a body of the United Nations, the International Criminal Tribunal for Crimes in the former Yugoslavia (known as ICTY) was established. Ethnic cleansing was described as genocide, which included massacre of unarmed civilians. Slobodan Milosevic was brought before a court in The Hague where in 2006 he died in prison allegedly from natural causes but amid rumours of poisoning. Other leaders arraigned included Ratko Mladić (known as The Butcher of Bosnia) who in 2019 was sentenced to life imprisonment.

CHAPTER SIXTEEN

THE OUTCOME

Anti-communist demonstrations – Yeltsin's first years – White House – Chechnya – election of 1996 – Yeltsin's health and death – corrupt financial deals – demise of communism – Marx's predictions unfulfilled – materialism irresistible – millennium impossible to achieve – communism prevalent today.

The failure of the hard-liners' coup in Russia, in the early 1990s, was followed by a wave of anti-communist feeling: statues of Stalin and other prominent communists were toppled and defaced; Lenin's embalmed body was removed from the tomb in the Kremlin; and the city of Leningrad resumed its previous name of St Petersburg.

Yeltsin took over Gorbachev's powers, assuming the title of president of the Russian Federation. He was soon to be in deep water. After seventy years of communism it was not possible for private enterprise and free markets to have immediate effect; unemployment increased and living standards were to decline rather than improve. Yeltsin was to lose his popularity and he clashed violently with the Russian parliament (known as People's Deputies), coming to a climax in 1993 when he ordered tanks to open fire on the parliamentary building known as The White House. He had come to power as a defender of liberty and democracy but he was to find that he had to resort to strong-arm violence on occasions, notably in combatting the province of Chechnya – Muslim, belligerent, and demanding independence ferociously.

During his rule of eight years Yeltsin went through hard times: his health was always precarious; besides intoxication he had to endure five heart attacks and a seven-hour quintuple bypass operation, but he was a survivor, somehow keeping going on painkillers and alcohol and he held office until his resignation in 1999. Against all the odds he had won a general election in 1996 partly because he was preferred to the communists who were his only plausible opponents, and partly because he had been able to initiate some revival of the Russian economy. His anti-communist stance had brought help from abroad and he had been boosted by unscrupulous financial deals with shady Russian entrepreneurs whereby state assets were privatised at give-away prices with some operators becoming inordinately wealthy.[46]

Yeltsin died in 2007 at the age of seventy-six. By then communism had fallen from grace. It had been shown conclusively that as a creator of wealth capitalism was infinitely superior. But there was more than just economics: communist doctrines had been shown to be unsound. Those propounded in the manifesto of 1848 – equalising of wealth, cooperation replacing competition, 'from each according to his abilities, to each according to his needs', sounded fine,

46 Enough to buy up English football clubs and prime property in such areas of London as Knightsbridge and Kensington.

but they had been subverted and appropriated by power-hungry tyrants to give moral tone to their tyrannical ways. None of Marx's predictions had been fulfilled: the proletariat of the world had not united in common cause against the bourgeoisie and had shown clearly that they would rather join the bourgeoisie than destroy it, and they preferred gradual social reform to seismic revolution. In times of war they were ready to fight on behalf of their country rather than for abstract idealism. Ultimately communism was undermined not so much by love of freedom and democracy as by materialism (or consumerism). The economy of expansion meant that such things as washing machines, television sets, motor cars and holidays in the sun became widely available and were welcome. Alexander Solzhenitsyn might plead that life with only physical pleasures and without spiritual values brought no lasting satisfaction, but such views were revered rather than practised.

The demise of communism was to underline two fundamental truths: that beliefs cannot be enforced on people with opposition stamped out and that it is beyond the capacity of humankind to create a kingdom of heaven on earth.

Tianmen Square, Beijing, scene of the last-scale anti-Communist protest in 1989 that lasted nearly six weeks and saw many thousand deaths.

ACKNOWLEDGEMENTS

In writing this book I have had invaluable help, notably from my cousin Priscilla Baines, ex-librarian of the House of Commons, who gave expert editorial advice. Also of great assistance was Delia Caple, typist par excellence and in Citysec well versed in business affairs; and as always there was full cooperation from the staff of the London Library.

I have not undertaken original research, relying entirely on secondary sources especially from the following: *A History of the Modern World from 1917 to the 1980s* by Paul Johnson (Weidenfeld and Nicolson, 1983); *The Secret War* by Max Hastings (William Collins, 2015); *The Spy and the Traitor* by Ben Macintyre (Viking, 2018).

INDEX